Back to Basic Selling

Back to Basic Selling

Unique sales tips for sure-fire success

Robert F. Taylor

A SPECTRUM BOOK

Prentice-Hall, Inc.,
Englewood Cliffs, New Jersey 07632

Taylor, Robert F.
  Back to basic selling.

  "A Spectrum book."
  Includes index.
  1. Selling. I. Title.
HF5438.25.T39 1985   658.8'5   85-6476
ISBN 0-13-056490-7
ISBN 0-13-056300-5 (pbk.)

Figure 5-3 used by permission of the Dartnell Corporation.

1 2 3 4 5 6 7 8 9 10

ISBN 0-13-056300-5

ISBN 0-13-056490-7 {PBK.}

Cover design © 1985 by Jeannette Jacobs
Manufacturing buyer: Carol Bystrom

This book is available at a special discount when ordered in
bulk quantities. Contact Prentice-Hall, Inc., General
Publishing Division, Special Sales, Englewood Cliffs, N.J. 07632.

Prentice-Hall International (UK) Limited, *London*
Prentice-Hall of Australia Pty. Limited, *Sydney*
Prentice-Hall Canada Inc., *Toronto*
Prentice-Hall Hispanoamericana, S.A., *Mexico*
Prentice-Hall of India Private Limited, *New Delhi*
Prentice-Hall of Japan, Inc., *Tokyo*
Prentice-Hall of Southeast Asia Pte. Ltd., *Singapore*
Whitehall Books Limited, *Wellington, New Zealand*
Editora Prentice-Hall do Brasil Ltda., *Rio de Janeiro*

Contents

Preface

This book emphasizes the importance of mastering the basic principles of selling on which to build an ongoing successful career in this field. These 123 field-tested tips contain specific and direct information helpful to the salesperson (both novice and veteran), sales manager, trainer, and educator.

Back to Basic Selling is unique because it presents ideas that are not usually taught in the average training class. They are offered in the style of a field sales manager coaching his representative on a "one on one" basis. The suggestions are brief, to the point, and easy to read and remember. They can be adapted to the personality and style of the individual—and put into practice with *immediate* and *favorable* results.

The salesperson who studies and practices these basics will definitely improve his or her performance and increase sales production; the sales manager and sales trainer will be more effective by teaching and using these productive tips; and educators will discover a "gold mine" of subjects that are ideal for the practical study of salesmanship.

These suggestions are *not* tricks or gimmicks. They are to be used in combination with quality products, good service, and ethical conduct.

In a competitive market, the salesperson who practices these ideas will surely have an advantage over the competition: His or her performance will make the difference when everything else is about equal. The sale is more easily made by the professional who presents the product to the market in the most effective manner. It is the "ensemble of professionalism" that provides the winning edge.

The "ensemble" is made up of many of the suggestions offered here. When these suggestions are put together and used in combination, they create an aura of professional confidence. Professionalism generates favorable attention and assures the buyer that he is dealing with a dedicated salesperson.

Many of these ideas are so basic that they are frequently neglected, resulting in weak and unsuccessful presentations.

The 123 sales tips were carefully evaluated and accepted only after crucial field testing. Only then were they integrated into sales presentations with successful, measurable results.

This book should become the handbook of sales representatives, managers, trainers, and educators. Its consistent use will:

1. Help new salespeople get into production faster—and with more profit and enjoyment.
2. Assist the experienced sales representative in freshening up his or her sales approaches and presentations.
3. Remind all salespeople of those basics that are so easy to forget.
4. Provide the sales managers and sales trainers with ideas for training and coaching.
5. Increase the sales productivity of salespeople.
6. Offer the teacher new subjects for salesmanship courses.
7. Enhance the profession of salesmanship and give it the respected image it deserves.

General Tips
on Salesmanship

Successful salesmanship is built on a solid training framework that consists of the following elements, or components:

1. Product knowledge
2. Markets and applications
3. Territory management
4. Time management
5. Sales techniques
6. Attitude

These general elements apply to all areas of sales training. This book gives *specific* tips in each of the six categories in the framework. This framework offers a logical sequence of instruction in the following:

1. *What* to sell (product knowledge).
2. *Where* to go to sell the products and *how* the products are used in each specific market (markets and applications).
3. *How* to organize and administer a sales territory (territory management).
4. *How* to execute the territory plans on a monthly, weekly, and daily basis (time management).
5. *How* to sell the products to the markets in the most effective way (sales techniques).
6. *How* to develop and maintain the power of enthusiasm in selling (attitude). Attitude can't be taught, but the right climate for good attitude can be provided.

Salesmanship is field generalship. It consists of planning, organizing, executing, evaluating, and modifying (when necessary). All of this requires training, which usually consists of corporate classroom training, field training, and self-training.

Large companies provide the initial training, usually at corporate headquarters. It is then continued (or should be) by field training, which also includes supervising and coaching. In addition (and of great importance), there is *self-training*. It is important for you to take the initiative in your own development.

Use the framework of product knowledge, markets and applications, territory management, time management, sales technique, and attitude as a guide to your self-training. It will serve you well when you review and evaluate your present operation, accept new items into your product line, work with your manager and peers, and train dealers and new salespeople. It will be a constant reminder that a well-balanced development program is needed. When all six major sections of the framework are used in combination, a successful sales program is easier to achieve.

As your company's representative in your territory, *you are in charge.* You are responsible for that piece of geography that has been assigned to you. It is a portion of the *whole company territory* that has been assigned to the vice-president of marketing to whom you report. Your successful handling of your territory plays an important part in the success of the company. The key to your success lies in your effectiveness at *the point of sale*. That is where the buyer's brain meets the seller's brain. The company's research, development, financing, manufacturing, and advertising are all aimed at success at *the point of sale*. That is where the product is converted back into cash with something left over called a *profit*.

This chapter is designed to give you a broad perspective on salesmanship. Keep it in mind as you perform as a salesperson in that important territory assigned to you.

RATE YOURSELF
ON YOUR SALES EXPERTISE

It is smart to take a close look at yourself and your strengths and weaknesses as a salesperson.

The two-page, self-rating form shown in Figure 1–1 will guide your thinking. It offers a broad view of many of the things a salesperson must know—and do. This form can serve as a self-improvement chart. You may wish to discuss your weak points with your sales manager. Together, you can work on the areas in which you need help.

Form the habit of periodically rating yourself (at least once a year). All professionals do it.

FOLLOW THESE STEPS
IN CONVERTING A SUSPECT
TO A PROSPECT TO A CUSTOMER

The conversion of a *suspect* to a *prospect* to a *customer* may take many steps. The completion of those steps may require many calls and considerable time. In some cases, however, the complete "conversion" can be accomplished in one call. A lot depends on the product or service being offered.

In either case, it is smart to keep this series of steps in mind. It will give you a good perspective of the work required to get the job done.

FIGURE 1-1   Self-rating chart

A SELF-RATING OF YOUR EXPERTISE IN PROFESSIONAL SALESMANSHIP

This rating form is offered as a means of determining (1) your strengths in certain subjects and (2) your needs for additional training.

The self-rating form will guide you to the sections of this book that are most important to you. It will also pinpoint your sales manager's training efforts in the improvement of your weak areas.

Therefore, please answer the following questions as objectively as possible.

	Are you strong in this area of training? YES or NO	Do you need help in this area of training? YES or NO
I. Product Knowledge Product knowledge includes the full product line, specifications, good features, technical details, pricing, scheduling, shipping, and servicing policies. It also includes similar information about competitors. In effect, product knowledge covers WHAT TO SELL and the terms and conditions. Comments:		
II. Markets and Applications This section covers the best markets for the products and the applications of those products in each market. Comments:		
III. Territory Management Territory Management means the study, organization, execution, and evaluation of strategic plans. These strategic plans are designed to (1) win a greater share of the market, (2) gain these increases at the lowest possible costs, and (3) deliver the greatest possible return on the investment of time, money and manpower. Comments:		

4

	Are you strong in this area of training? YES or NO	Do you need help in this area of training? YES or NO

IV. Time Management

Time Management is the careful planning of the sales day, the sales week and the sales month. It is the disciplined execution of those plans. It is the best and most profitable use of each available sales hour. Time Management covers the TACTICS needed to carry out the strategic plans of Territory Management.

Comments:

V. Sales Techniques

These Sales Techniques are ones employed for the planning, organizing, executing and evaluating the presentations of the products to the markets in the most efficient and productive manner. It includes the development of new business and the controlling of established accounts.

Comments:

Here are some sub-sections of Sales Techniques

1. "People Selling" as Well as Product Selling
2. Face-to-Face Selling
3. Selling by Telephone
4. Selling by Mail
5. Selling by Formal, Written Proposal
6. Finding the "Right" Man
7. Getting Appointments
8. Pre-approach Planning
9. Approaching the Prospect or Customer
10. Gaining Favorable Attention
11. Developing a Dialogue
12. Making the Proposal
13. Handling Objections
14. Getting the Desired Action
15. Servicing the Account

Comments:

_____
Signature

5

The steps for some prospects may not follow exactly in this order. For example, the demonstration could precede the survey or proposal. (See Figure 1–2.)

FIGURE 1–2 Steps to convert a suspect to a prospect to a customer

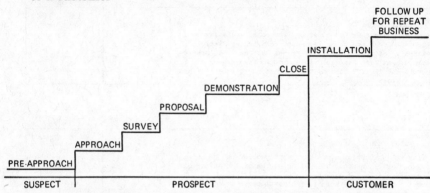

The completion of these steps in the conversion process may take a number of calls—either face-to-face or by telephone. It is smart to plan each of these calls to get the greatest benefit from them. There are two formulas for such preparation. One is called the AIDCA formula. In every contact you:

A. Get the *attention* of the prospect or customer.
I. Create *interest* in you and your objective for that call.
D. Create the *desire* to learn more about that objective.
C. *Convince* the prospect to proceed as you wish.
A. Get the *action* desired.

A second formula frequently used in place of AIDCA is:

1. Gain favorable attention.
2. Develop a dialogue with your prospect or customer.
3. Make your proposal (your objective for the call).
4. Handle objections to your proposal.
5. Get the desired action.

As in the conversion steps, the sequence of events in either of these two formulas may not occur in the order listed. The two formulas simply serve as reminders for planning each call as you work from suspect to prospect to customer.

USE THE FOUR METHODS
OF CONTACTING A PROSPECT
OR CUSTOMER

There are four ways for you to get your sales message to your prospect or customer. They are:

1. Face to face
2. By telephone
3. By mail
4. By formal, written proposal

Use all four in combination whenever possible. The face-to-face sales presentation is usually the most effective. As your good judgment dictates, use the other three to precede or follow your face-to-face call.

Use the telephone to set up an appointment, and use it after the face-to-face call to convey additional information, check the results of your call, request a second appointment, keep your proposition "hot," or ask for the order.

Use the mail prior to the call to generate interest and prepare the way for an appointment, and use it after the call to thank the prospect, convey additional information, and maintain the sales momentum you built up in your face-to-face call.

Use the formal, written proposal when your prospect says: "Put something in writing and I'll take it up with management."

All four contact methods will be covered in greater detail in later chapters of this book.

In addition to the four methods of contact for you to use, your company may provide others, such as the following:

T.V advertising
Radio advertising
Direct mail
Magazine advertising
Trade shows
Billboard advertising
Newspaper advertising
Yellow pages

These are powerful adjuncts to your personal sales effort. Use them in combination with your four contact methods. It will make your selling job much easier.

FEEL GOOD ABOUT YOURSELF
AS A SALES REPRESENTATIVE

- You are a very important person.
- Your company cannot successfully operate without salespeople.
- Our country cannot remain as a superpower without salespeople to sell its national production.
- Your prospects and customers cannot operate without the consultative advice of suppliers' sales representatives.

Why are these four statements true? They are true because the industrial cycle is made up of a series of continuous events. It is like a wheel that never stops turning. It starts with the invention of the product or the creation of a service; then the financing of the project; then the manufacture of the product; and then the conversion of the product back into money. The money is reinvested in research and development, purchasing supplies, manufacturing more products, making more sales and producing earnings to the company, dividends to the stockholders, and income to the workers and salespeople.

The conversion of the product back into money is the function of *marketing*—and *salesmanship* is a vital part of that marketing thrust. As a salesperson, *you* perform a key role in that industrial cycle. Your work is necessary in the whole scheme of things. Your function of selling is of equal importance to that of financing, purchasing, storing, manufacturing, and shipping.

As an important sales professional, you can perform a vital function, make a lot of money doing it, thoroughly enjoy the fun of selling, and be highly respected in your company and community.

BE AN ACTIVE MEMBER
OF THE SALES TEAM

You will have more fun and enjoy profitable returns when you enthusiastically participate as a member of your sales group.

Each member of a sales force has certain strengths—and some weaknesses. A good sales supervisor plays on the strengths of his people. Those individual strengths, when put together, create a synergistic effort: The total is greater than the sum of its parts. That enormous power is there for each group member to tap and profit from its use.

Such action, however, works both ways. You must *give* as well as receive. You must contribute your strengths for the benefit of your team. You may think: "I don't have any particular expertise." On the surface, that may appear to be true when you think of expertise as coming from years of experience. Even though you are new in selling and don't possess much sales background, you have native intelligence—and perhaps a natural instinct for selling. Therefore, as you participate in the group discussions, you can offer smart (and perhaps original) ideas for sales tactics and tools. When this happens, all members of the group benefit—and so do you. *You* gain an immeasurable return on your investment of ideas because:

1. You have concentrated on the problem.
2. You exercised your native intelligence to help solve the problem.
3. You contributed something—which gives you enormous psychological benefits.

4. You win a high status in your organization. This, in turn, encourages your team members to offer you tips and tools from their own arsenals of successful techniques.

Make sure that you thoroughly understand the objectives—as well as the job description—of your sales supervisor. You play a vital role in the achievement of his goals and the fulfillment of his responsibilities. Therefore, you must know what they are. Unfortunately, many sales managers don't confide these things to the sales representatives. It is easy for your boss to take for granted that you know what he is trying to accomplish. It is up to you to get the full perspective of the duties and responsibilities of your boss and the objectives of your sales team.

Only then can you get an accurate view of *your* goals and *your* responsibilities to *your* sales group. You realize that you play an important part in the overall plan. You understand that if you don't carry your share, it then places an additional burden on your fellow salespeople.

Give and you will receive.

SUGGESTIONS FOR GOOD HUMAN RELATIONS

The suggestions in this section apply to relations with your fellow workers as well as your customers.

Developing and maintaining good human relations should be done routinely by all caring individuals. Your purpose, however, is more than altruistic. Following the rules for good human relations is just *good business*. It is a psychological fact that humans tend to reciprocate in a similar manner. They will react favorably to good treatment—and unfavorably to bad treatment. A customer will respond to good service by giving you repeat orders. A colleague will respond to your friendly assistance by helping you in return.

Go out of your way to meet people in your own and other company departments. Make a point of being friendly to people in your customers' departments.

Be active in professional organizations. Membership in the SWAP Club and Sales and Marketing Executives, for example, will put you in contact with many people with similar interests. They can help you and you can help them. (The SWAP Club is a national organization of salespeople. The chapters hold breakfast meetings and "swap" sales leads and ideas. Sales and Marketing Executives International is an organization based in New York City.)

Make routine phone calls to your colleagues, friends, and customers. Maintain those precious relationships. Show people that you care.

Don't be a "loner." Selling can be a lonely business unless you work at developing and maintaining good relations with your prospects, customers, and colleagues.

Here are some rules for human relations:

1. Treat others as you would want to be treated.
2. Be generous with your praise of others.
3. Be sincere.
4. Keep your word. If you promise to do something, do it!
5. Call people by name. (Learn the names of principals *and* subordinates—and speak to them by name.)
6. Smile.
7. Listen intently—and show that you are *really* listening.
8. Care for others—and show it.

HELP YOUR SALES SUPERVISOR HELP YOU

Your boss is a very important person in your life. He can help you to become a better salesperson. *But you've got to help him do it.* There's a reason for this.

Chances are your sales supervisor was a good salesman before he was promoted. But, as is frequently the case, he became a star salesperson by using certain methods and sales techniques that came naturally to him, and you can tap that tremendous store of knowledge for your own improvement. But it isn't easy to get him to teach you. The reason is that he learned many of those techniques by sheer instinct. He said and did the right things in sales situations *without really thinking about what he was doing—and why.*

11

This background of field experience doesn't necessarily make him a good coach and teacher. He may assume that everyone has the right "gut" feeling for successful techniques. He may take it for granted that you don't need help in "how to sell"—and therefore he doesn't offer it.

You can solve the problem by asking him questions. They can be simple questions on things that are bothering you, such as:

How did you call a prospect for an appointment?

Did you call a customer for an appointment or just drop in?

How did you find "the right man"?

What did you do and say when you got a "put off"?

What are the advantages and disadvantages of a cold call?

What type of briefcase did you use and how did you use it?

How did you show a sales brochure to a prospect without losing control of the interview?

What did you do to reduce driving and waiting time?

What is a good "batting average" of calls to sales?

What is a good ratio of prospect calls to customer calls?

Did your call on a prospect differ from one on a customer?

What call planning tools did you use?

In the case of my _____ prospect, what benefits should I emphasize? What are some good "selling sentences" for this prospect?

What are some good closing questions to use?

Such questions will almost force your supervisor to analyze his own methods and understand why they were used and why they were successful. In effect, you help him *dissect* his past triumphs. A powerful pattern of persuasion can be developed from that playback. With it, he becomes a better coach and teacher—and you profit as his pupil. You help him help you.

ENCOURAGE COACHING
BY YOUR SALES MANAGER

One of the usual responsibilities of the sales manager is the coaching of his or her salespeople. The job description for the first-line sales manager is written something like this:

> *The primary function of the district manager is to improve sales production in a given geographic territory. This will be done by training, supervising, and coaching all sales representatives under his or her command. Sales can be dramatically improved by training each representative to become better organized, more efficient, and more productive. Supervising and coaching will ensure the correct implementation of the training. This training, supervising, and coaching includes experienced as well as inexperienced sales representatives.*

> *The district sales manager will continue the training initiated by corporate headquarters. He or she will teach, supervise, and coach following the programs and using the materials supplied by corporate training headquarters.*

> *In general, the district manager is responsible for the following:*

> 1. Improving sales and profits in each territory.
> 2. Coordinating the entire sales efforts for the district.
> 3. Continuous training and development of all personnel within the district.
> 4. Implementing company policies and directives.

Training, supervising, and coaching by the sales manager is designed to help you improve your sales production. Training provides you with the knowledge and techniques you need for successful selling. Supervision and coaching will ensure the correct application of that training. Supervision by your sales manager includes the observation of you and your peers as you perform your sales tasks.

Coaching is a more direct, one-on-one function. The sales manager watches you work and then discusses with you the good and poor features of your presentation. In discussing the good points, he or she tells you why they were effective. In critiquing the parts that are not so good, he or she will tell you why they were not effective and how to improve them.

Most coaching sessions are held in the field immediately after each call, and then in a general summary at the end of the day. (Some coaching can be done in the office when planning and preparing for the day's work.)

The prime purpose of coaching sessions is to strengthen the skills of the salesperson. (It is *not* to afford the sales manager the opportunity to demonstrate *his* selling skills.) The coaching process, therefore, is for your benefit. Indicate to your sales manager that you want him to make calls with you—that you want his advice. Such assistance will be helpful to you—and it's a good way to build rapport with your boss.

CAPITALIZE ON
YOUR PERSONAL IMPACT

Salesmanship is more than just selling products or ideas. Professional salespeople know that they must also sell themselves. With everything else being equal, individual personalities have to make the difference.

The total impression you make on others is called *your personal impact.* That impression or impact can make the difference for you—either positively or negatively. A bad impact can lose the sale even though your product is superb, a good impact can make the sale even though your product is the same as your competitor's.

Buyers, like other people, are human and impressionable. They respond, just as we do, to good and bad impressions. Personal impact is the complete picture of yourself that you give to others through your dress, appearance, deportment, body language, and selection and delivery of words (vocabulary and speech).

The picture the buyer is looking for is one that expresses sincerity, assurance, friendliness, appreciation, trustworthiness, stability, and success. To make the right impression on that buyer, your personal impact must convey all those things by the following:

The right selection of clothing

Your posture

Your walk

Good eye contact

Sincere smile

Appropriate head nods

Rewarding remarks

Follow-through on commitments

Sincere "thank yous"

Look at yourself as others see you. How do you come across to your peers and prospects? Consider how you can favorably influence others by an improved personal impact—and then work on it.

MAKE YOUR COMMITMENT TO EXCELLENCE

There is an increasing demand in the business world for quality performance. Men and women in business are becoming more and more conscious of the need for excellence—in their product, service, and customer relations.

Excellence in product and service is not enough. It must be accompanied by excellence in customer relations. For example, a gruff, surly mechanic can do an excellent job of repairing, but his poor customer relations can alienate the customer.

Salespeople must respond to this rising demand for excellence. They have no choice: Customers will give their business to the salespeople who are obviously dedicated to the creed of excellence. The *search for excellence* has become a crusade in many organizations. The salesperson

15

must develop and maintain a continuous effort for excellence—to match that of many of his customers.

Excellence in performance can be described as "doing it right the first time." For the sales representative, that could mean the following:

- Doing the right planning for the call.
- Making the right approach to the prospect.
- Making the right presentation for that particular sales situation.
- Following up commitments in the right manner.
- Giving the account the right service.

The dictionary definition of "excellence" is: "of great virtue or high quality, extremely good;" And the definition of "perfect" is: "without defect or blemish."

In the business world it is almost impossible to be perfect in every contact and transaction—but it *is* possible to be excellent.

The right attitude generated when striving for excellence will be demonstrated in the following:

- Correcting a mistake quickly and courteously.
- Servicing the account promptly and efficiently.
- Handling the irate customer in a fair way and on a win–win basis—both buyer and seller win.

The right attitude will go a long way in satisfying the customer and maintaining repeat business. You will make more sales, maintain your established business, get more referrals, earn more money, and be happier on your job by having your own crusade for excellence.

DON'T BECOME TOO SATISFIED
WITH YOUR SALES PERFORMANCE

This suggestion is directed to the older, experienced salesperson; however, its message is valuable to *all* salespeople in various stages of expertise.

Don't become too satisfied with your sales performance. Don't adopt a "know it all" attitude. Don't ever believe that you know everything there is to know about selling: It's possible that you can profit from new ideas and fresh techniques. Always be on the alert for any new information that can improve your professionalism as a salesperson.

There is nothing new in this suggestion. People in all professions do it: They study the techniques of others; they read books and attend seminars; and they follow a continuous course in self-improvement.

It is very easy to reach a plateau in your sales production and earnings. This is especially true with people who have their major obligations behind them—such as children's educations, home mortgages, marriages, and all those motivating challenges that made them sharp and aggressive as salespersons.

Several things happen when you become satisfied with a plateau in your sales performance and earnings:

1. Your sales manager is presented with an embarrassing problem.
2. Your fellow salespeople become critical of your self-satisfied approach to your job responsibilities.
3. *Something happens to you.* You develop a secret, inner feeling of dissatisfaction with yourself. It is a subconscious awareness that your attitude and conduct is wrong—that you are being unfair to yourself by not working up to your maximum in job performance. These deep signals to yourself sometimes surface in different forms, such as:

   - Cynicism about sales training.
   - Overassertiveness at sales meetings.
   - Impatience with "naive" questions or suggestions presented by newer salespeople.
   - An Olympian attitude expressed by tardiness and early departures from the job, fewer calls, indifference to company problems, and only placid support of company sales objectives.

No company nor sales manager can tolerate a "plateau syndrome" in an employee. One of three choices will have to be made:

1. A termination or early retirement.
2. A reduction of territory.
3. An attempt to change the salespersons attitude and help him to recognize the danger of the "plateau," both to him and the company.

Chances are your manager will prefer the third choice but will not know how to go about it.

A "plateau" state of mind does the salesperson more harm than it does the company. The very instincts that made you a top performer—a successful salesperson—are the same instincts that are now telling you: *Use those sales talents; share them with others; help your fellow salespeople; get back on the team;* and, at the same time, *start again that sales production that made you a star over the years.*

You will be rewarded by a satisfying psychological return on your investment.

Tips on Product Knowledge

Product knowledge is the bedrock of all sales training. You must know *what* to sell before you learn *how* to sell it.

Almost all companies do well in product training. They provide product manuals, brochures, and specification sheets. It is the obvious thing to do—and it is the easiest part of sales training.

Company information is also provided. The corporate image is a "product" in the sales sense. The company's reputation for quality, research and development, financial strength, and long service in the industry are all good features. They play an important part in presenting the physical product to the market. Product information also includes pricing, scheduling, shipping and warehousing facilities, warranties, and service policies.

All this material forms the basis for "Feature–Benefit Selling." (This is discussed later in more detail.)

Product training is usually given at the company's factory or in field classes. It includes product demonstrations and technical descriptions—all supported by written material and illustrations.

Your training in the product knowledge area must also include similar information about competition. You must know everything possible about your competitors. This is called *market intelligence,* and you can't be a professional sales strategist without it. If your company doesn't provide it, you must get it by yourself. The method is similar to military intelligence.

Most companies have good features and poor features in their products, services, prices, and policies. It is smart to know them all—both good and bad. You will then be able to present the good features (in terms of benefits) and be prepared to cope with objections to the poor features.

The following tips are offered to supplement the product information already supplied by your company. They require self-training—which, in turn, demands some initiative, dedication, and self-discipline.

ANALYZE THE FEATURES OF A PRODUCT

Features are products, components, services, prices, and policies. When put into use by the buyer, they provide either benefits or losses. They are therefore designated as either good features or poor features. The chapters of this book that cover sales techniques will help you translate the good features to benefits and the poor features to losses. This is known as *feature–benefit selling.* It is built on a solid foundation of product knowledge.

Here are some examples of good features:

good quality	power steering
accuracy	reasonable price
speed	complete inventory
strength	capacity
durability	economy

long wear
efficiency of manufacture
expertise of the backup team
quality control
variety of sizes
variety of packages
telephone calling system
trained delivery personnel
accurate delivery schedules
emergency delivery service
superior quality
reasonable terms
research and development
years of good service
reliability
manufacturing plants
   nearby
fair pricing

prompt shipment
new design
sharp edge
hydraulic power
sanitation
"spot check" system
market studies
co-op advertising
P.O.P. assistance
"on loan" props
low capital investment
all sales guaranteed
corporate image
financial strength
handsome profits
member of local business
   community
large fleet of trucks

Here are some examples of poor features:

poor quality
slow rate
low durability
high prices
incomplete inventory
low capacity
delayed shipments
bald tires

inaccuracy
weakness
obsolete design
inefficient manufacture
distant warehouses
high cost
dull edge

As you study *what* you have to sell, also consider *how* you are going to sell it. For example, as you are taught to strip and reassemble a product, concentrate on each component. Ask these questions:

Why is it built this way?
How does the competition build theirs—and why?
What are the advantages of our product over theirs?

The same dissection method should be applied to pricing policies, service and shipping facilities, warranties, corporation structure, and corporate image.

21

Some of the answers to your questions may not be in the company manuals. This is where initiative and self-training are needed. The answers you seek are available somewhere in your company or public library.

The Product Analysis form shown in Figure 2–1 can be used for analyzing an item in your product line. Select a familiar product—one that you have already "dissected." List its features. Think of those features from the viewpoint of a prospective buyer. Think, also, of the nearest *competitive* product. In terms of the prospect's needs and in comparison with the competitive product, are your features good or poor? Put a check mark for each feature in the appropriate column.

ANALYZE THE FEATURES
OF COMPETITIVE PRODUCTS

This tip is a continuation of the preceding one. It is designed to help you think clearly and objectively about competition.

Select a competitive product that is similar to your own product—for example, the one you analyzed in the preceding section.

Follow the same analysis procedure. Use the second Product Analysis form shown in Figure 2–2. List all the features of that competitive product. Keep in mind the viewpoint of the prospective buyer. Also, compare *your* product with the competitive product. As you list each feature of the competitive product, ask youself this question:

> In terms of the prospective buyer's need, is this a good feature or a poor feature?

Mark the appropriate column.

ANALYZE YOUR *FULL* PRODUCT LINE

This tip will assist you in developing a broad perspective of your complete product line. Remember, the word *product* in this context means all the other things you sell besides the physical products. This includes features such as company

FIGURE 2–1 Product analysis form for your product line

PRODUCT:

Features of the Product	Good Feature ✓	Poor Feature ✓

FIGURE 2–2 Product analysis form for your competitor's product line

PRODUCT:

Features of the Product	Good Feature ✓	Poor Feature ✓

24

reputation, research and development facilities, pricing, service and warehouse facilities, warranties, service policies, and quality performance.

You may have a number of products in your line. If this is the case, select only the *principal* features of each one.

Once again, think in terms of:

1. The needs of the prospective buyer.
2. The complete product line of your strongest competitor.

As you list each feature, ask yourself this question:

Is this a good feature or a poor feature?

Using the Analysis of Complete Product Line form shown in Figure 2–3 mark the appropriate column.

PRACTICE WITH YOUR PRODUCTS AND STUDY YOUR COMPETITION

Become proficient in handling, operating, and demonstrating every item in your product line.

Work closely with your fellow salespeople in the development of the fastest and most polished operating techniques. (You can have fun with races and speed tests.)

Make friends with users of competitive equipment. Those relationships will pay enormous dividends because:

1. You will learn about the competitor's good features and poor features.
2. You will have the opportunity to sell *your* product when the time is right.

Take every opportunity to attend trade shows and exhibits where you can inspect new state of the art products in your industry.

Read trade magazines that will keep you posted on trends and developments.

FIGURE 2–3 Analysis of a complete product line

Principal Feature	Good Feature ✓	Poor Feature ✓

MAINTAIN CONTACT
WITH YOUR COMPANY SERVICE PERSONNEL

Service people frequently know more than salespeople about the company product line. Take advantage of that knowledge.

Maintain good relations with the service personnel. Encourage them to tell you of chronic service problems. This is especially important when *your* customers are involved.

This friendly, open communication with the service people will do the following:

- Keep you alert to serious faults with your equipment.
- Prepare you for calls from irate customers.
- Encourage suggestions for better operating techniques.
- Alert you to possible new equipment sales.
- Coordinate sales and service with each account.

Tips on Markets
and Applications

The study of markets and applications is a logical step after product training. In fact, in many cases some market and application training is given *during* product training. It is natural for a salesperson to ask: "Who buys this and how is it used?" The answer to that question begins the training on markets and the application of the product in each market.

A company's markets should be classified into two groups:

1. Existing markets
2. New markets

Many companies enjoy a wide distribution to many markets. In many cases the *use* of the product is common to almost *all* markets. An example of that is the paper clip.

Other companies suffer from a very narrow existing market. The use of the product is the same but the markets are limited. An example of that is the railroad car wheel.

A company is sometimes forced out of business because its existing market disappears. An example of that is a buggy whip manufacturer.

Some companies can continue to grow by changing their perspectives early enough. For example, a buggy manufacturer with a much broader concept of the transportation business would meet changing times by going into other means of transporting people and goods before his product became obsolete.

Within the existing markets are companies that are *prospects*—not customers. For example, a company that sells testing equipment to steel mills has sold *some* mills but not *all*. The need for testing is common to *all* steel mills. Therefore, the nonuser steel mills are prospects to that manufacturer of testing equipment.

Here is another example. An enterprising salesman for a duplicating machine manufacturer learned that architects have a common need: *Their specifications had to be duplicated*. The number of copies needed depended on the size of the project. The salesman first consulted his branch office customer records to determine how many architects were customers. He then checked the Yellow Pages under "Architects." After checking off the customers, the names remaining were those of prospects. He proceeded to sell the prospects the duplicating equipment they needed.

Companies must be constantly alert for every opportunity to:

- Get a greater share of existing markets.
- Find additional applications to existing markets.
- Develop new markets.

As the manager of your territory, you must also be searching for new customers, new applications, and new markets. Your alertness could help you increase your sales. It could also open up new horizons for your company. The following tips will help you.

USE THE S.I.C. CODE
TO PINPOINT YOUR PROSPECTS

You can save a lot of time by pinpointing your sales targets. Use a "rifle"—not a "shot gun"—approach to your territory management.

The S.I.C. (Standard Industrial Classification) code will help you zero in on the most likely prospects—and economize on those precious "contact" hours.

The S.I.C. is a system of business coding initiated by the federal government. It can be found in every manufacturer's directory. There is a directory for every state in the union. Almost any public library has one in its business section.

The S.I.C. includes every type of business establishment by code number. A quick way to take advantage of this valuable information is to look at your own company's customer records. List, by S.I.C. numbers, the key customers who are presently using your company's equipment and supplies in quantities. Then investigate the applications of your products in those industries. Chances are that other companies in those select classifications have the same needs and applications for your products.

The next step, then, is to refer to the manufacturer's directory and list all the nonusers in those select classifications. That list gives you the names of select prospects. By the very nature of their business and the history of success with similar companies, you know that these nonusers could use the same service. This program of selecting key targets follows the principles of efficient, professional marketing strategies.

The source information is available to you. By using your initiative and doing some "homework," you can increase your sales production with the minimum expenditure of time and money.

PRACTICE THE "MANAGEMENT BY EXCEPTION"
TECHNIQUE WHEN STUDYING
MARKETS AND APPLICATIONS

Many directories contain a numeric list of manufacturers and processors by the S.I.C. They also contain:

- Names of establishments classified by products, including some other business organizations rendering services to manufacturers and businesses at large.
- An alphabetical index of manufacturers and processors by company name in geographical sections.
- Geographical listings of manufacturers and processors listed by city or town with telephone address and mailing address, plus key information on personnel, products, size, and worth.

The key information includes the names of the officers, products, S.I.C. code, and the number of employees.

In almost any directory 90 percent of the companies listed have fewer than 100 employees. Now you can apply the Management by Exception technique. Confine your first stage of market study to the remaining 10 percent (the largest accounts). This suggestion does not imply that some of the smaller companies (fewer than 100 employees) are not good prospects. It makes sense, however, to concentrate first on the big ones and take care of the others later.

Follow the suggestions contained in the preceding tip. By linking what you know about applications to S.I.C. classifications, you have zeroed in on your most promising markets.

Later, follow the same procedure for the companies that have 50 to 100 employees. Then, if your product is right for small accounts—and if time permits—work on those small organizations. This is a good way to get the job done faster and more profitably.

APPLY THE MARKETS AND APPLICATIONS TIPS TO A SPECIFIC CASE

To make sure you understand the tips on markets and applications, it is suggested that you apply these ideas at once. The best ways to learn is to study, apply what you've learned immediately, and evaluate the results.

For the moment, concentrate your attention on one of your most important customers (a user of your product).

Determine the S.I.C code of that customer.

Describe the application of your product by that account.

Find a prospect (a nonuser) that has the same S.I.C. code as the selected customer. (Consult the numeric list of S.I.C.s in the manufacturer's directory.) Chances are that the prospect has the same applications as your customer.

Call on the prospect and discuss his needs in terms of applications.

This type of pinpointed prospecting will certainly increase your chances of success in obtaining new business.

UNDERSTAND THE PRODUCT APPLICATION BY YOUR CUSTOMER

Ask questions when you call on customers. Find out how they are using your product—and the benefits they gain from that use.

From what you know about similar businesses, make sure your customers are aware of *all* the applications that are practical for that product.

You will be pleased with the increased business it brings you.

Then call on prospects of the same classification and spread the good news. Tell them how your customers have benefited. Use testimonials and success stories.

You will get a greater market penetration, more sales, and increased income.

Tips on Territory Management

Territory management is the employment, on a territory level, of many of the same principles used on a national and international level. It requires the study, preparation, execution, and evaluation of strategic plans. These strategic plans are designed to do the following:

1. Sell a greater share of the market.
2. Increase sales at the lowest possible cost.
3. Achieve the greatest possible return on the investment of time, money, and manpower.

Territory management covers the strategies needed for efficient territory coverage. Time management (discussed in Chapter 5) includes the *tactics* needed to carry out the *strategies* of territory management.

The following list contains terms that are commonly used in the study of territory management:

Potential. The potential of an account is the maximum volume that can be used by the customer or prospect. This applies to county, sector, or complete territory possibilities. The potential is the total volume sold by a company and all competitors in a given area. It is sometimes referred to as "the total market."

Current market share. The company's present volume in ratio to the total potential in the territory of the account.

Market penetration. Same as *Market share.*

Account penetration. The percentage of an account's potential you are currently selling.

Pivot points. Strategic positions in the geographic territory. They can be the home of the sales representative and his office, the shipping points, or key customers and prospects. These pivot points serve as centers of sales activities for the day or a sales trip. The sales representative pivots his sales work from these key points.

Work load. The time (sales man-hours) required to effectively cover the customer and prospect. There is only a limited number of contact hours available in the sales year. It is important, therefore, to allocate the work load for an account, a county, a sector, and the total territory. As the territory manager, you are expected to plan, implement, control, and evaluate action in the following major segments:

1. The analysis of the total potential in your geographic territory.
2. The review of your present market share.
3. The study of the strategy and tactics of the competition.
4. The research of key influences, present and future, that must be taken into account.

5. The review of lost business and the reasons for it.
6. The logistical analysis of the territory. This will include the locations of shipping points and pivot points, and the sectors and counties containing the greatest sales opportunities.
7. The classification of customers and prospects by potential volume.
8. The analysis of your present account penetration.
9. The work load analysis by account and by call frequency.
10. The evaluation of the quality of salesmanship.
11. The analysis of the cost involved in covering an account.
12. The modifications, if necessary, of the work load and cost analysis. These changes may be necessary to correspond to the maximum hours available—and the returns on invested time and expense.
13. The setting of goals for the territory and sectors.
14. The establishment of measurement tools for the evaluation of progress made in achieving the goals.

In effect, you have a continuous, five-pronged program of territory management created to do the following:

1. To *maintain* your present volume from established customers.
2. To sell *additional* products to those existing accounts.
3. To sell *"in depth"* to other divisions of existing accounts.
4. To sell your competitors' customers.
5. To find and sell new accounts and new markets.

This is a "capsule" course in territory management. It is offered as a supplement or reinforcement to the training program provided by your company.

The following tips on territory management will give you some "how to" ideas to help you perform your functions as your company's territory manager.

CLASSIFY YOUR CUSTOMERS AND PROSPECTS BY THEIR POTENTIAL

Classify your customers and prospects by "A," "B," and "C" groups. This classification is based on the potential (not the current volume) of each account. (Note: The dictionary definition of "potential" is: "possible, expectable.") The possible and expectable volume from an account is comprised of your sales of your products, your competitors' sales of similar products, plus the possible additional use of those products in the various departments and divisions of the account.

Your classification procedure includes prospects as well as customers. The final summary of all "A," "B," and "C" prospects and customers then gives you the estimated total potential of your territory. This classification method helps you to determine your primary and secondary goals.

Your first goal is in two parts:

1. To sell the maximum volume to your "A" *customers*.
2. To sell the maximum volume to your "A" *prospects* (new business). Note: In many cases it is easier to sell additional volume to your *present* customers because of the relationship already established with those friendly accounts.

Your secondary goal is to cover your "B" customers and prospects. This goal is also in two parts:

1. To sell the maximum volume to your "B" *customers.*
2. To sell the maximum volume to your "B" *prospects.*

The potential for your "A" prospects and customers is greater than that for your "B" accounts. Your "A's" will in most cases take priority over your "B's" in your strategic planning.

The third classification—the "C" customers and prospects—is of less importance because the sales opportunities are smaller. (In some cases the sales costs could exceed the profit from those accounts.)

Coverage of the small accounts can be integrated into your routine for the "A's" and 'B's." Your infrequent calls on the "C's" can be interspersed by telephone and mail coverage.

MAINTAIN A STRATEGIC MAP AS A TERRITORY MANAGEMENT TOOL

As a territory manager, you must do the same type of study that your vice-president of marketing does at corporate headquarters. He has a strategic map of the whole country. He knows that there are more than 3000 counties in the United States. He knows the buying power of each of those counties. He studies in detail the *type* of business in them, highlighting with colors the strongest and weakest counties (in terms of potential for your type of business). From those studies, your top management knows where to place branch, district, and regional offices—and where to place salespeople. This is putting the sales coverage where the action is—or should be.

The corporate studies also include the cost of sales. Your top management knows the approximate direct cost of "mining out" sales from each county. They may decide to ignore some of the counties because the cost of sales would be in excess of the value from those orders. An example of this practical analysis is in the mining industry. There are lodes of lead, silver, and gold unmined in remote mountain areas. The cost of "mining out" is prohibitive in ratio to the value of the ore.

Follow the example of your vice-president of marketing. Develop a strategic map of *your* territory. It will reveal to you, at a quick glance, your basic coverage problems. It will help you develop your strategic plan for efficient, effective sales operations.

If you have a large geographic territory, get a state road map. If you cover more than one state, use a road map for each state. If you have a small geographic territory (perhaps a six-block-square city territory), draw a large, rough map of it.

Mount your map on corkboard or cardboard. With a heavy marking pen, draw the outline of your territory. With a different color marker, draw the outlines of the counties. (For a small city territory, draw the outline with one color and the city blocks or postal zones with another.)

Use colored pins to designate the locations in each county/territory of your "A," "B," and "C" customers and prospects. (For a brand new territory, or if you have not classified your "A," "B," and "C" accounts, use the Buying Power Index. It will give you the buying strength of each county. It can be purchased from Sales & Marketing Management, 633 Third Avenue, New York, New York 10164.)

In the business section of most public libraries, you can get any information you need from directories such as Thomas Register and Dun's Registers. You will also find a manufacturer's directory for your state. This is particularly helpful because it gives the following:

> Name of the company
> Address
> Telephone number
> Names of principal officers
> Number of employees
> Financial strength
> S.I.C. code
> Type of product manufactured

Use this map for planning your sales coverage. Follow the principle of Management by Exception. Concentrate on those "A" prospects and customers as much as you can. Those are the ones that will yield the greatest return on your invested sales man-hours.

GOAL SETTING

Goal setting is an important part of strategic planning. It is exactly what is being done at corporate headquarters on national and international levels. It is a natural setup that follows mapping and routing.

Goal setting for your territory will help direct your sales efforts. A frequent review of your goals will keep you on track. It will also be an excellent training exercise as you prepare for a promotion. Your superiors must set goals every six months, and it is good for you to follow their example.

Without clearly defined written objectives, it is easy to become diverted from the main goals. A typical sales day, sales week and sales month can be filled with minor distractions—many must be attended to. But while you are doing that, keep your eye on those original goals you set. They will serve as "beacon lights" to keep you on course.

Also, setting goals—and then achieving them—has a powerful, positive effect on your morale. Your frequent reviews of your progress will "psych you up" and spur you on toward even greater achievements.

Your primary goal is greater market penetration—in other words, to sell a larger share of the potential. You can put that goal into measurable terms, such as:

> I shall gain a 10 percent increase in sales within the next twelve months.

But to arrive at that primary goal takes some work. It involves the development of *sector* goals. Sector goals are designed to achieve the *primary* objective. The market penetration goals for all sectors of your geographic territory ensure a realistic approach to the setting of the primary goal. Your main objective is simply a total of the sector goals.

Developing sector goals is not easy: It takes some work and some deep thinking. (Deep and objective thinking is what strategic planning is all about.) The sector goals are derived from your plans for selling to the individual prospect and customer. In other words, you set a goal for *each* account by:

1. Considering your present volume being sold to that account.
2. Knowing the potential of that account.
3. Weighing your chances of selling a better percentage of that account's potential.

4. Arriving at a realistic sales volume objective for that account during a twelve-month period.

Your sector goals, therefore, are made from your account objectives, and your primary goal is the sum of all sector goals. This careful and detailed study ensures a realistic approach to a measurable primary goal.

DEVELOP A ROUTING PLAN FOR TERRITORY COVERAGE

Your territory map is your basic tool for developing efficient routing plans. You have marked the locations of your "A", "B", and "C" accounts.

Now plot on the map your "pivot points." Pivot points are your office, your home, your shipping points, and some of your major customers and prospects. They are the locations from which you start your sales day.

Now the facts are all there on the map. Stand back and take a good look at it. Many of the routes from your pivot points are pretty obvious. You have probably already established some and are currently using them.

Here are some suggestions that will be helpful in improving your present routes or establishing new ones:

1. The proximity to a shipping point gives you a powerful advantage over your competition. Use a shipping point as the center of concentric circles (see Figure 4–1). Make sure all important customers and prospects are well covered within those circles. Your nearness to the shipping point gives you a winning edge in terms of lower shipping costs and easier deliveries. Sell all that can be sold within those circles.

2. Divide your territory into sectors for practical routing (see Figure 4–2). The locations of the sectors must, of course, be governed by the road and highway system.

3. In a strategic position within a sector, you may wish to select a certain hotel as a temporary pivot point and message center to be used as you work that sector.

4. Your routes should always include a good mix of "A" customers and prospects.

FIGURE 4-1

FIGURE 4-2

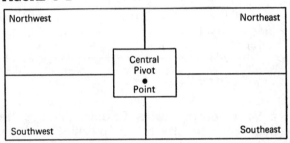

5. All routing plans should include ways and means of reducing driving time during those valuable "contact" hours.

   A sales day consists of the following:

   a. Hours in which it is practical to call on customers and prospects. These are normal "contact" hours.

   b. Very early morning and late evening hours in which it is not feasible to call on accounts. These are "noncontact" hours.

   There are many things that a salesperson can do as well, if not better, during those noncontact hours. One is the driving time to the first call and from the last call. Good routing will keep that "dead" time to a minimum. There are several types of routes that may be practical in your territory: One is the "cloverleaf" routing, and the other is the "straight line" route (see Figure 4–3 and 4–4).

6. A major objective for your routing should be the frequent coverage of those territories where the potential is greatest. In other words, work the territories in which you have the best opportunities for increased business.

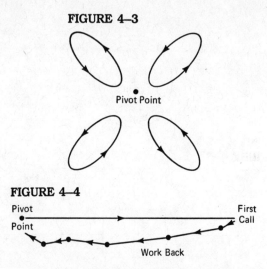

FIGURE 4–3

Pivot Point

FIGURE 4–4

Pivot Point

First Call

Work Back

7. Keep your routing plans flexible. Change them as needed. With that strategic map visible and up to date at all times, you will know the roads and the locations of your major accounts and prospects. You can change course as new selling opportunities arise.

ANALYZE THE WORK LOAD
FOR EFFECTIVE TERRITORY COVERAGE

For most sales representatives, there are only 2082 contact hours in the entire year. It is smart to allocate those contact hours to customers and prospects that will yield the greatest return on your invested time. It is recognized that such allocation cannot be "carved in stone." Emergencies are bound to crop up that will force a change of plan. It is good strategy, however, to think of your territory coverage in terms of workload. A workload analysis is usually made by routes—and by customers and prospects on those routes.

Start with your most important prospects and customers (the "A" accounts). Consider them one at a time. Answer the following questions:

1. How much time do I need for one sales call on this account? (Note: For customers, remember that you

have two assignments for every call: (1) to hold the established business and obtain repeat orders, and (2) to sell additional items.

2. How much time must be spent driving to that account from the last call?
3. How many calls should I devote to this account during the next six months?

Add the "call time" (#1) to the "driving time" (#2), and multiply by the number of calls (#3). Mark the total hours on your record for that account. Follow this same procedure for *all* prospects and customers on that route (or sector of your territory). Do the same for all the routes or sectors in your territory.

Compare the grand total of estimated hours to the total number of contact hours in the six-month period. If your workload estimate exceeds the total contact hours for six months (about 1040), revise your estimates. Start with your "C" customers and prospects, and reduce the number of sales hours assigned to them. Perhaps telephone and mail contacts with "C" accounts can be substituted for some of the face-to-face calls.

Such a workload analysis will emphasize to you the great importance of allocating your time to the "A" and "B" accounts. There are just so many contact hours available— you can't make any more. So, make the best use of the ones you have.

INCLUDE INTERMEDIATE CONTACTS BY MAIL AND TELEPHONE

Strategic mapping and routing places great emphasis on the "A" and "B" prospects and customers. There are only 2082 contact hours in the selling year. Therefore, some of the "C" customers and prospects must take a lower priority in the regular selling schedule.

Some portions of the "C" account coverage can be handled by mail and telephone. Similarly, intermediate coverage of your "A" and "B" accounts should be part of your strategic plan. It is important to keep your name in the minds of your clients in the periods between your in-person contacts with them.

These intermediate contacts can be easy, informal chats by telephone and via friendly notes by mail. They are powerful supplements to direct contacts. Your greatest asset is your image as a consultative salesperson. Demonstrate your sincere desire to help your account. Drop in the mail tidbits of useful information accompanied by a friendly, informal, personal note. Find good reasons in terms of benefit to the customer for calling your accounts by telephone. Make your calls brief, to the point—and worthwhile to the customer.

Intermediate contacts by telephone and mail will maintain that momentum you have built up in your sales calls. They will demonstrate to your clients that you really care about them.

USE "DOOR OPENERS" TO FIND NEW PROSPECTS

Be ever on the alert for new prospects. Use every possible sales tactic in your continuous search for new business. Advertising, mailings, and telephoning are some of the traditional "door openers" to new accounts. Use them. In addition, take advantage of your good reputation with your satisfied customers. They can be effective door openers.

Customers who are enthusiastic about you, your product, and your service will be eager to help you. They will receive a psychological "lift" by recommending you to others. Testimonials and references are vital to your sales success. They open the doors to new sales horizons.

But it isn't easy to win the enthusiastic endorsement from customers. It takes hard work and dedication and it demands the consultative type of selling. It requires good selling and *good service* after the sale is made.

Customers are hungry for super service that ranges far beyond the normal follow-up. They are unhappy with the typical "sell 'em and leave 'em" attitude that is so prevalent. To properly service your account, you must really care about your contacts there. You must want them to get the best possible results from the purchase. The enthusiastic response and testimonial from your satisfied customer is in almost equal ratio to your investment of time and service.

Continue to use advertising, mailings, and telephoning as door openers. Those methods are good if properly used. But the most effective door opener is the recommendation by a friendly, satisfied customer. When you approach a prospect with that—or, better yet, when he contacts you—the sale is already half made.

BE PREPARED FOR THE OCCASIONAL SALES SLUMP—AND HANDLE IT

Let's face it. Selling isn't always exciting and rewarding. There are bad times as well as good times. A rising sales curve is fun to look at day after day. A plunging sales line—or even a level one—is depressing and discouraging. That discouragement can create a chain reaction and an even greater decline in sales.

A sales slump can be caused by one thing or a combination of things. It can be from a recent event (such as the loss of a key account). It can also be the result of bad sales tactics over a period of time (such as neglect of accounts or poor customer relations).

Here are some suggestions to follow if you hit a sales slump:

1. Review your sales call reports. Do this objectively.
   a. How many calls have you made during the last three months?
   b. What percentage of those calls were on prospects?
   c. What was your average number of calls per day?
2. Review your sales volume for the same quarter.
   a. What was your average sales production per call?
   b. What percentage of your sales volume was from new accounts?
3. Review your customer records. Were there any significant changes in the buying patterns of established accounts?

4. The review of your sales calls and sales production may reveal some faults that you must correct at once. For example, it is easy to spend too much time with established accounts at the expense of new business development. It is also easy to rationalize the need for paperwork in the office during a sales day.

5. Change your sales routine. Work a part of your territory that you may have neglected.

6. Freshen up your sales presentation. Practice before a mirror and with a cassette player. Clean out your briefcase and your car. Restock them with fresh sales materials.

7. Stay out of the office for three or four days (call in from the field). Concentrate on prospect calls.

An honest diagnosis of your present sales operations might reveal some faults. The correction of those faults will pull you out of your sales slump.

A periodic and objective evaluation of your sales activities might reveal some bad sales tactics. You can then make early improvements—thus preventing the sales slump from happening in the first place.

USE A MEMO FILE
TO MAINTAIN EFFICIENT RECORDS
OF YOUR SALES CONTACTS

Every sales call creates details such as commitments, dates, questions to be answered, and follow-ups. At the end of the day, some of those details can be easily forgotten.

It is smart to capture those items onto some form of memo sheet. The best time to do that is immediately after the call while those details are fresh in your mind. (Note: the same applies to telephone calls.)

Please refer to Figure 4–5. The Memo form is one that has been found very useful to many salespeople. It can be used before and after the face-to-face call and telephone call. It can be filed alphabetically by customer name (see the file in Figure 4–5) and retrieved very quickly as needed.

FIGURE 4–5 A memo form and memo file.

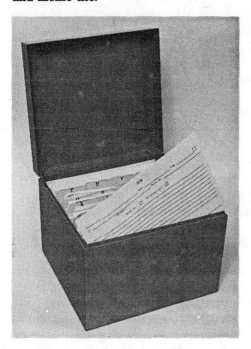

```
                              MEMO
Talked with _____ Date _____ Time _____
Of _____ Phone No. _____
                  (Company)
                  Sales Call [ ]    Telephone Call [ ]
Address _____
My objective _____
_____
_____
Results _____
_____
_____
Action or follow-up necessary _____
_____
_____
```

The file and a good supply of memo blanks can be carried in the car for use during the day. It is easily portable so it can be brought in at the end of the day for final completion and review for the next day. Additional memo sheets for the same customer can be stapled together with the most recent memo on top. Many salespeople color-code their memo sheets: red for "A" accounts, yellow for "B" accounts, and blue for "C" accounts.

This method is important to the salesperson. It takes self-discipline to keep it up, but it is worth it. Total recall is sometimes vital to the success of a sale. A simple sheet of paper can prevent a possible disaster.

SELL THE FULL PRODUCT LINE
—AND SELL "IN DEPTH"

A very common error salespeople make is to sell only a portion of the full product line. Another common mistake is to sell only one department and neglect the customer's other units.

It is easy to fall into the habit of pushing favorite products and to overlook opportunities for the sale of others. Don't make that mistake—you are missing a good bet if you do. Capitalize on the good relationship you have with your customer. In subsequent calls on him, gradually open up your full product line. He deserves to be shown everything you have to offer, and you deserve the sale of additional items. In some cases you can increase the dollar value of your order in a single call. That is called "selling the full line."

"Selling in depth" is slightly different from "selling the full line." It means selling to the other departments and divisions of the account. Frequently, if asked, your customer will refer you to prospective buyers in the other units.

Take full advantage of your good work with the first division. Ask for names and needs in the other divisions. It will start a chain reaction from satisfied users. Eventually, you will have sold all the divisions that need your service or products.

Tips on
Time Management

Time management covers the tactics used to implement the plans and strategies of territory management. It covers the tasks performed during the sales day, sales week, and sales month. It concentrates on the time conservation tactics that will help you get the job done faster, better, and with more profit to you. Poor time management is one of the most common causes of failure in selling.

Time management is interlocked with all the other segments of a well-planned sales program.

1. It goes hand in hand with product knowledge because time can be wasted by presenting the wrong product—or being unable to provide the necessary product information.

2. It is closely linked to markets and applications because the salesperson is directed to the right market and to

the prospects with the greatest potential, thus helping him or her make the most economical use of time.

3. It is vital to the success of sales techniques; and, conversely, good sales techniques are important in time management because a well-planned and effectively executed sales call is a timesaver.

4. You employ tactics to carry out the strategic plans of territory management.

In summary, good time management means spending every possible minute in contact with prospects and customers. It means making every one of those minutes count toward more sales and better earnings. It involves the use of the noncontact hours for nonselling tasks. Good time management provides the maximum contact hours for presenting your products to your markets in the most productive manner.

The following tips on time management will offer some fresh ideas that will help you be most effective as a time manager—and territory manager.

TAKE MAXIMUM ADVANTAGE OF ALL CONTACT HOURS

The average salesperson has only 2082 selling hours per year. These are the normal business hours in which most sales contacts are acceptable. We know, of course, that some business relationships will permit sales calls in "off" hours, such as early in the morning or in the evening.

There are more noncontact hours in the business year than there are contact hours. (Please refer to the "A" and "B" sections in Figure 5–1.)

The professional salesperson tries, as much as possible, to reserve the contact hours for selling tasks. Whenever possible, he performs the nonselling tasks during the noncontact hours. The nonselling assignments should be such things as writing call reports, planning the next sales day, loading the car, preparing sales tools, and writing letters.

We know, of course, that some contact hours must be spent on nonselling jobs such as driving from one call to another and waiting for the prospect. Careful planning, telephoning for appointments, and lobby tactics can reduce the wasted time during the contact hours. The form Things to Do Today, provides space for assigning tasks to contact and noncontact hours (see Figure 5–2). This daily planner sheet can guide your thinking so that you get the most productive use of your selling time.

FIGURE 5–1   Chart of contact and noncontact hours

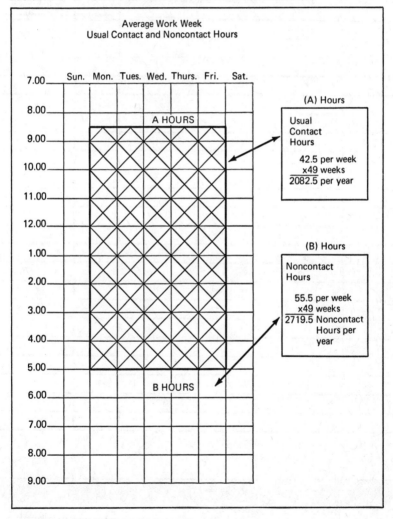

FIGURE 5–2 "Things to do today" form

Priority Number	To Be Done Today	A During Contact Hours	B During Non–Contact Hours
	Date _____		
	Things to do today		

PLAN YOUR TIME
BY MONTH AND BY DAY

Your selling time is precious. Use it wisely. Work by appointment whenever possible, and plan your month and selling days. Use action planners—there are many versions on the market. The Dartnell Action Planner is especially good for planning for months ahead (see Figure 5–3).

A homemade version of the monthly planner is the simple Time Planner sheet (see Figure 5–4). This sheet can be photocopied to provide twelve copies for the full year. Each monthly copy is marked by the days of that month. The blank squares can be used for miscellaneous notes.

The sales month can be fine tuned into detailed planning for each day and hour. The Day-Timer is an excellent tool for that purpose (see Figure 5–5). The Day-Timer set for the full year contains a file box and twelve monthly units. The salesperson carries two units with him (for the current month and the following month).

These simple sales tools are vital to the professional. They help plan the day and month—and then help you work the plan.

FIGURE 5–3　Monthly planner book

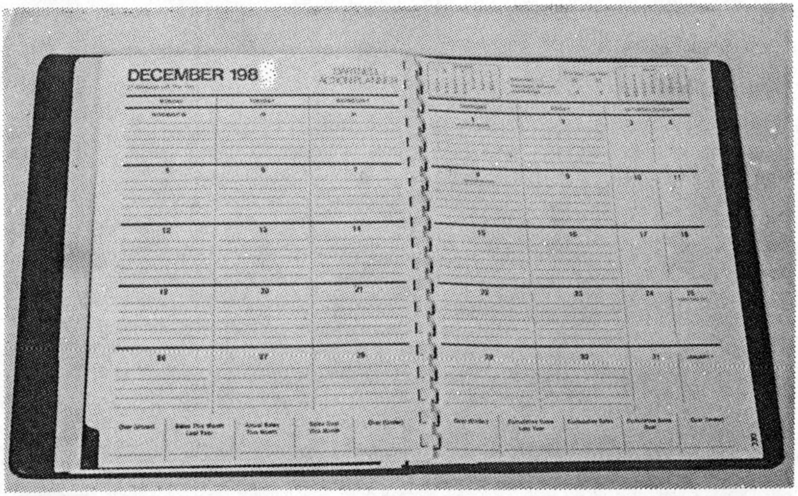

FIGURE 5—4 Daily time planner sheet

MONTH_____, 19__

SUNDAY	MONDAY	TUESDAY	WEDNESDAY	THURSDAY	FRIDAY	SATURDAY

FIGURE 5–5 Day-timer file and day-timer book

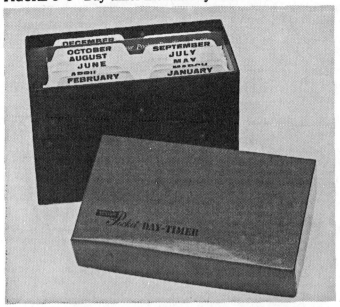

WORK BY APPOINTMENT WHEN POSSIBLE

It is a good idea to "frame out" each sales day with appointments. You will be better organized when you make commitments in advance—and then keep them as scheduled. This practice is a form of self-discipline—as well as good time management.

Appointments are also good for the prospects because it allows them to prepare for your coming. Your telephone call for an appointment is a sales call. You must sell the appointment. Like the sales call itself, the telephone call must be planned to make the prospect want to see you. (An example of a telephone call for an appointment is given in Chapter 8, "Tips on Telephone Techniques.")

MAKE YOUR CAR YOUR MOBILE OFFICE

Your car is your "office away from your office." You use it to carry you to your prospect's parking lot. You leave your mobile office to enter your prospect's place of business. In addition to a means of transportation, your car is a traveling warehouse of supplies, sales brochures, and visual aids. From that warehouse you stock your briefcase with the materials you need for a particular call. If that mobile office is properly stocked, you never lack for exactly the right material for each call.

The best time to load your car is during the noncontact hours, during the evening before the sales day. This is when you can really concentrate on the next day's work and the supplies you will need. You can then be confident that you are well prepared—and adequately stocked—when you start out for a full day of effective selling.

One of the most efficient ways to stock your car is by the use of a portable file. It can be carried in the trunk of the car or on the back seat. It doesn't have to be a heavy, expensive file. There are excellent cardboard files (such as the Banker's Box R-Kive) that can be purchased in almost any stationery store. File folders can be hung from a built-in steel frame to carry your selection of brochures and materials. A well-planned, carefully stocked file is insurance against lost sales that could be caused by missing items.

Your mobile office also contains your "desk." For example, a small, portable memo file next to the driver's seat provides notes for the upcoming call and blank memo forms for reporting the completed call.

Think of your car as a mobile office. Stock it carefully. Use it wisely. It will pay enormous dividends.

AVOID "TIME WASTERS"

Be aware of the common time wasters—and avoid them whenever possible.

A time waster is an activity that is nonproductive in terms of sales. Some time wasters are obvious—such as long lunch hours and coffee breaks. Others are not so obvious. For example, it is easy to rationalize long waits in customers' lobbies.

Your contact hours are precious and should be used as much as possible for profitable sales production.

Here are some typical time wasters:

- Frequent call-backs on small accounts.
- Poor handling and rehandling of paperwork.
- Long waits in lobbies.
- Excessive driving during contact hours.
- Not working by appointment.
- Unnecessary conversations with prospects, customers, and colleagues.
- Poor planning of sales interviews.
- Forgetting important sales tools.
- Not selling the full line to each account.
- Making personal calls when telephoning would suffice.
- Poor preapproach work in territory analysis.
- Inefficient routing of sales calls.
- Conducting personal business during contact hours.
- Inefficient use of the mail to supplement personal calls and telephoning.

- Planning the sales day during contact hours.
- Loading the car during contact hours.

Make a list of the less productive work (time wasters) you have done—or have seen done by others—during contact hours. Keep the list handy for the next two or three weeks. Add to your list as you check your own operations and observe other salespeople in action.

Continue to ask yourself: "Is this the best use of my time right now?" When you are constantly on the alert to time wasters, you will learn to avoid them. Your sales production and earnings will increase. You will become a true professional.

EXCESSIVE USE OF ALCOHOL CAN BE A TIME WASTER

In many cases, social drinking is part of the selling world. It is accepted at sales meetings and in customer entertainment. When used wisely, it can be an adjunct to the rapport-building process, although many successful salespeople do well without it.

Excessive drinking can be seen at almost any sales meeting during the cocktail hour. It is impossible to calculate how many budding careers have been ruined by bad behavior caused by too much alcohol.

Each person has an alcohol tolerance. Some people can't handle even one drink; others can take two or three drinks without "letting the bars down." It behooves you to know your fine line of tolerance and respect it. Even moderate use of alcohol can be a time waster. When taken during the lunch hour, for example, it can slow you down for the afternoon's sales work.

For the salesperson, the most damaging use of alcohol is excessive drinking during the evening when on a business trip. It frequently results in late hours and not enough sleep. This, in turn, causes a slow start and even illness the following morning. When you have a "bad night," you can be certain that the following day will be lost. This is an expensive time waster.

It is unfortunate that the average sales manager does not speak frankly about excessive use of alcohol, but he or she does expect each salesperson to use plain common sense. Some representatives do and some don't. Good common sense concerning alcohol can separate "the men from the boys."

MAKE THOSE LONELY HOTEL STAYS CONSTRUCTIVE

Nights away from home on business trips can be profitable. With none of the usual family interruptions, you can get a lot of things done in your hotel room. The hours between dinner time and bedtime can be used to enhance your career as a professional salesperson. For example, you can do the following:

1. Summarize and evaluate the day's work.
2. Plan your work for the following day.
3. Study sales and sales management courses.

After a long sales day, it is always smart to write reports and make notes of commitments made. Many details can escape you when you wait to do this upon your return home.

It is also very smart to plan in detail every call you expect to make on the following day. This is professional salesmanship. It is also good psychology. At wake-up time the following morning, you will look forward with pleasure to those well-planned calls.

It is always good to do some reading and study for your present job and for advancement. Evenings away from home are lonely, but you can make them constructive and profitable.

BEWARE OF THE "HEAD NODDER"

In your sales work, you call on a variety of types of people. One type that can waste a lot of your time is the "head nodder." This is the agreeable person who makes you feel welcome, agrees with everything you say, acts enthusiastic—but never buys.

It is easy to be mislead by the head nodder. You get frustrated by the daily turn-downs and put-offs, so the friendly head nodder is a welcome relief. It is tempting to classify him in your reports as a "hot prospect." He *is* friendly, but he certainly isn't hot. Don't let him waste your time by making call-back after call-back on this type.

Find out early in the game if the head nodder is likely to buy—and when. Do this by *asking* him—politely but bluntly. A question such as: "You agree that this is a good product and that you need it. Do *you* have the final authority to buy or will there be others involved in the purchase?"

That question tells him that you are there to sell. If he replies by saying that his authority is all that is needed, ask the next question: "When shall I ship?"

If, instead, his answer is that another person must be involved in the purchase, ask an alternative question: "Is it okay with you if I contact him directly—or should we go in together to see him?"

The answers to these questions will soon reveal to you whether you do indeed have a prospect—or just a time waster.

Tips on
Sales Techniques
for All Types
of Contacts

This chapter is devoted to those tips on sales techniques that apply to all four types of sales contacts with customers and prospects:

> Face to face
> Telephone
> Mail
> Formal, written proposal

Subsequent chapters will concentrate on those tips that are *specific* to each of the four types of contact.

The sales techniques portion of *any* sales training program covers how to sell the product to the market in the most effective manner.

Sales techniques are the tactics employed to achieve the objective of every contact. They are applied when working with customers as well as prospects. To be successful, sales techniques must be used in combination with product knowledge, markets and applications, territory management, time management, and attitude.

The ideas presented here will augment those offered in your company's training program. They are techniques that are frequently overlooked in many corporate programs.

The major portion of this book is devoted to sales techniques. That is because without the right sales technique, all your training in the other areas will be less productive.

Apply these ideas to your selling style and personality. It will improve your sales production.

PRACTICE THE PSYCHOLOGY OF PERSUASION

Some products are so unique and the need for them so vital that they "sell themselves." Conversely, other products are similar—if not identical—to those of your competitors. They require the efforts of professional salespeople. In other words, the salespeople make the difference; it is salesmanship that provides the winning edge.

Salesmanship is the art of determining the prospects needs, making sure the product will fill those needs, proving it, and completing a transaction that is mutually satisfactory to both the buyer and the seller. To accomplish this, the buyer must be sold on both the product and on the seller of that product. The seller must be pleasing as well as assuring to the buyer, and the buyer responds by wanting to do business with that particular salesperson. This is why the psychology of persuasion is important to the sales representative. Psychological principles, linked with professional presentations, will definitely improve the salesperson's batting average.

The basis for the psychology of persuasion is social interaction. Social interaction is the process by which people influence other people through the mutual interchange of thoughts, feelings, and reactions. We see it every day in our business and social lives.

The importance of a satisfying social interaction between the seller and the prospective buyer is best described by the words "assuring" and "pleasing." The buyer must be assured (made certain) that his deal with the seller is good for his company and for himself. One of the greatest fears a buyer has is that a bad purchase (perhaps involving quality or delivery) could bring personal criticism on him; or create losses of time, money, and delays for his company.

In addition to being assured (feeling safe), the buyer will be much more inclined to place an order with a salesperson who pleases him than with one who doesn't.

Techniques for pleasing and persuading used in social interaction are built on the urges or needs of human nature.

- The need to be needed.
- The need to be wanted.
- The need to contribute something.
- The need to be important to other people.

When one person fills a basic need of another, the receiver gains a thing of value and is instinctively impelled to reciprocate in kind—to give something of value in return to the one who has filled that need. Translating that into selling language: If your buyer receives something he wants and needs from you, he is instinctively motivated to give you what he perceives you want and need.

In psychological language, the word "value" covers areas far beyond the normal interpretation of the word. "Value" can be dollar value, such as cost savings to the buyer or an order to you. "Value" to the prospect can also include many other things, such as:

- Favorable reaction to your appearance.
- Pleasant relationship with you, the seller.
- Ease of understanding.
- Appeal to pride.
- Feeling of importance.

- Favorable reaction to your obvious respect for him and his time.
- Enjoyment of the dialogue.

When you and your prospect are face to face, something more than communication is going on; not only information but "value" is being exchanged. For example, when the prospect receives something of value from you—even something small like a smile, good eye contact, a nod of the head, or a rewarding remark—he is impelled to reciprocate by giving something of value, such as:

- More information concerning his problems.
- Willingness to spend more time in the discussion.
- Agreement to a survey of his present methods.
- Agreement to buy your product or services.

Similarly, body language, the use of visual aids, the use of testimonials and success stories, and the smooth handling of sales tools are all of psychological value. The assure the prospect of his understanding, and they please him because of your professionalism.

Involve your prospect in dialogue. Ask questions, indicate sincere interest in the buyer as a person, solicit opinions, make rewarding remarks, listen intently, and signify your agreement and use the paraphrase. Do what comes naturally based on plain social perception.

A good way to check this out is to study your own reaction to people. (Psychologists say that the way to understand people is to first understand oneself.) Ask yourself: "How do I react to the good listener, the friendly smile, the concise, pictorial explanation of a proposal, and suggestions worded in terms of benefits to me?

Your self-examination will make it easier to understand the human factors of the persuasion pattern being used every day by thousands of successful people. They are successful in human relations—and in selling. In fact, selling is human relations.

SELL PEOPLE AS WELL AS YOUR PRODUCT

People buy with their hearts as well as with their heads. Little (seemingly insignificant) things influence them for or against the product, the seller, and the seller's company. Don't ever forget that. Your planned sales presentations must always include people selling as well as product selling.

Psychologists have recently studied the common characteristics of the top performers of hundreds of sales forces. They discovered that most of those star salespeople excel in social interaction—the ability to engage a prospect in dialogue. They do this through the use of probing questions early in the interview to search out the prospect's needs, as well as to determine his mood.

This social interaction helps to gain the favorable attention that is so vital in the initial stages of the contact with your prospect and customer. After you have developed a good presence and pleased the prospect, the stage is set for determining his needs—and your sales job is well on its way to success.

FOLLOW A BUYER'S ADVICE
FOR SALESPEOPLE

To be successful in sales, we must always keep in mind the viewpoint of the buyer. The word "buyer" includes customers as well as prospects. The following advice for salespeople—derived from a survey of buyers—will help you as you prepare your sales presentations.

1. Know as much as you can find out about me before you make your contact with me.
2. When we meet (or make contact by telephone), don't tell me about *you*, but start immediately talking about *me—my* interests, *my* convenience, and *my* profit. Tell me how I might sell more and make more profit.
3. Remember that selling is done with the head *and* the heart; therefore, use care not to offend. I may dislike smoking and smoker's breath, so use social tact. Figure out how to please me—not displease me. I have been known to let my heart rule my head.

4. Tell me about your product and services, but translate it in terms of my needs and my objectives. Tell me these things in terms of benefits I can derive from the good features.

5. I may, at some point, want to tell you how far you have progressed with your sale and what more you can do to get the order—so you had better listen when I talk.

6. If I am your customer now, keep probing for additional needs and you'll see many opportunities to sell me additional items to the one we currently buy from you.

7. Don't take my business for granted. I may fool you. Work as hard to hold my business as you did to get it— and your competition will do the worrying. Always keep in mind that your *customer* is your competitor's *prospect*.

8. I want you to be loyal, but I don't expect loyalty at the expense of your company, for it is then robbed of its true worth.

9. Finally, in my book a good sale to you is a good purchase to me. A worthwhile transaction is a bilateral contract in which both parties benefit. I prefer to do business with a salesperson who presents the proposition as one business person to another and with the confidence born from knowing the offering is a good deal for me.

When your seller's brain meets the buyer's brain, keep these nine points in mind. You will be pleased with the favorable response.

"PROGRAM" YOUR BRAIN
WITH EXPLORATORY QUESTIONS

The *question* is an important tool for the consultative salesperson. You cannot work as a creative professional until you determine the prospect's needs. This is accomplished by establishing a dialogue. The dialogue isn't just idle chatter— it is a give-and-take discussion, and the principal burden is on you. You must keep the conversation flowing by shrewd questioning. (Those questions are prepared in advance, and are designed to dig out information about the prospect, his needs, his company, and his company's needs.)

It is smart to "program" your brain with carefully planned questions. It is also smart to take notes of the prospect's replies to your questions. Those replies form the basis for your proposal. In effect, your questions reveal needs and your proposal suggests ways to fill those needs.

The best type of question for determining the needs of your prospect is exploratory. It is an open-ended question that cannot be answered by a simple "yes" or "no" Some of the best salespeople start with the traditional What, When, Where, Why, Who, and How questions.

Here are some examples:

What is the biggest problem in your _____?
For example:
- sales force
- factory operations
- supervisor's training
- sales training
- management development
- When does this happen?

Where do you find immediate service when you need it so desperately?

Why do you feel so strongly about that?

Who is responsible for that condition?

How could that be corrected?

All questions must be accompanied by good listening and body language to indicate intense interest. Remember to "program" your brain with well-planned questions. It's good salesmanship.

USE THE "REWARDING REMARK" AND "PARAPHRASE" TO MAINTAIN DIALOGUE

The dialogue (the social interaction between buyer and seller) is an important part of the sales interview. It greatly differs from the sales pitch or monologue in which the sales-person simply tells the sales story without interruption.

In the dialogue, the buyer and seller discuss needs, problems, and solutions. To do it right, the salesperson uses some very common social techniques. One is the *rewarding remark*. It assures the buyer that the seller is "with him" and agrees with him. It encourages the buyer to continue the dialogue with simple comments such as "Right," "Fine," "That's great," "You're so right," or "I see." The rewarding remark is accompanied by body language such as the smile, head nod, good eye contact, and leaning forward to indicate interest. This combination creates a easy, relaxed climate that is conducive to good selling.

Another technique for maintaining dialogue is the use of the *paraphrase*. This is a simple, everyday tactic used to please the prospect. The paraphrase is a repetition of the prospect's recent statement, either in his exact words or your own interpretation of those words. By saying "Mr. Brown, a moment ago you said that . . .," you are not only reinforcing the buyer's words, but you are also giving him a psychological value. By remembering what he said and how he said it, you are making him feel important—thus motivating him to act favorably to you and your suggestions.

Be alert to the tactful use of the rewarding remark and the paraphrase. These techniques will encourage dialogue—and that is good salesmanship.

USE NAMES TO GAIN FAVORABLE ATTENTION

A person's name is music to his ears. Make a note of the name of each people with whom you come in contact on the way in and out of a prospect's office. For example, when calling a prospect for an appointment and the secretary answers the phone, say: "Is this Mr. Wilson's secretary?" And then when she answers "Yes," you say very respectfully: "What is your name, please?"

Make a note next to Mr. Wilson's name on your tele-phone index. Place the secretary's name in parentheses next to Mr. Wilson's name, and in subsequent calls, call her by name. You will be pleasantly surprised how she will help you get additional appointments. Confide in her. Tell her your mission and give her a chance to help you. Call staff assistants by name and treat them with respect. They can help you or hinder you. One never knows when a lower ranking staff person can come into power.

When to Go
On a First-Name Basis

Be careful about using first names too soon. Let the prospect and his staff members set the pace. As a general rule, continue to address the prospect by his last name for several interviews after he has started to call you by your first name (or nickname). The same applies to his staff assistants, with the possible exception of his secretary.

You will be able to determine how to address the prospect's secretary in your initial contact with her. When you ask "What is your name, please?" the reply will be either "My name is Agnes," or "My name is Agnes Barton." If you get the first reply, proceed immediately to address her by her first name. Her reply has indicated that the informality is okay. If you get the second reply, call her Ms. Barton until she suggests that you call her by her first name.

Use the Name
to Signal a Change of Pace

As you proceed through the various stages of a sales interview, use the prospect's name to indicate the advancement from one stage to the start of another. When you address him by name, you will alert him to the change. Some examples follow.

1. After the usual "small talk" at the beginning of the interview, say something like this: "Mr. Russell, my company has made many successful installations for other companies in your industry. May I ask you some questions about your operations?" (The use of Mr. Russell's name is the signal that you wish to get down to business.)

2. After you have handled some objections and want to start the close summary, say: "Mr. Russell, let me sum up my proposition. . . . "

REMEMBER THE RULES
FOR REMEMBERING NAMES

Dale Carnegie said, "One of the best ways to win friends and influence people is to remember their names."

You will stand out as a true professional when you call your prospects and their associates by name. It is smart to greet even the lowliest subordinate by name. It's a great "pleaser"—and it's good sales psychology.

To remember names, you have to work at it. It isn't easy. It takes concentration—and the sincere desire to please others by remembering their names.

There are certain common-sense rules to follow for remembering names.

1. *Be sure to hear the name.* So frequently names are given too casually—and indistinctly. Don't be afraid to ask for the name to be repeated. You won't offend. In fact, you compliment a person when you indicate that his or her name is important to you. If possible, write the name. This is easy when you're on the telephone with writing facilities available. If actual writing is not convenient, *imagine* yourself writing the name. If it is a difficult name, spell it phonetically.

2. *Repeat the name.* Repeat it slowly and distinctly so that the other person (a) *knows* that you have it, (b) has the opportunity to correct it if you have it wrong, and (c) is pleased that you really *want* to know his or her name.

3. *Observe the other person's prominent features.* Every person has certain features that can be associated with the name—shape of the chin, the eyes, shape of the head, hair style, race, shape of the face, ears, and neck. This takes concentration, which is one of the keys to good name recall.

4. *Engage the person in conversation.* During a brief chat, use the name several times. Determine some facts about the person—his job, hobby, favorite sport, and any other information that can be tactfully obtained. Repeat the name to yourself—linking the name to the facts.

5. *Record information about the person.* For long-term retention of the name, write the facts about a person on a memo form. This is especially important for your customer records. Suppose, for example, your customer is a purchasing agent who has a staff of four people. Accumulate and record the names, distinguishing features, interests, and assignments of *all* four people. Call them by name when you visit the purchasing agent. If possible, engage them in brief chats. Mention special subjects you remember as of particular interest to them.

Following these five rules for remembering names will pay enormous dividends. Your investment of time, concentration, and fact finding will make you stand out. Customers and prospects will be impressed with you and will find ways to reciprocate.

WATCH PEOPLE—AND LEARN

Be a "people watcher." Concentrate on the buyer; listen to his words and observe his body language. Develop a "built-in radar." Be a watcher of yourself. Use body language to signal messages to the buyer and to reinforce your verbal presentation.

You must understand the buyer and sense what's in his mind. You do that by hearing the buyer's words and observing his body language. Is he signaling tension, disinterest, doubt, acceptance, boredom, time pressures, lack of knowledge, and so on? Seventy percent of the buyer's message is conveyed through his body language. Likewise, seventy percent of *your* message is communicated through your body signals.

Many new salespeople are self-conscious. The definition of *self-conscious* is being conscious of one's self. It is almost impossible to be self-conscious and conscious of the other person at the same time. Therefore, concentration on the buyer will help solve the problem of feeling self-conscious. Learn to concentrate on the buyer, his words, facial expressions, tone, hand gestures, and posture. You will soon develop a "built-in radar." You will be so alert to the cues he is giving you that you will forget to be self-conscious.

Be more aware of your body language. Practice your sales presentation before a full-length mirror. Watch your body language and use it to emphasize your key points. Your body language can work for you and make you stand out, or it can work against you. For example, in replying to your prospect's objection, you can antagonize him by smiling, responding too hastily, and acting overconfident. Instead you pause, look thoughtful, stroke your chin, and then reply in a clam, assured manner even though you have heard that objection ten times today. Your facial expressions, hand gestures, and posture work together in a "cue cluster," indicate great respect for your prospect's opinion as well as strong belief in your proposition. Good eye contact is particularly powerful. Use it frequently during the sales interview.

Be a watcher of people. You will understand them better—and your own body language will improve. You will be a more effective salesperson when you become a better observer.

HELP YOUR PROSPECT RECALL SOME PROBLEMS WITH HIS PRESENT SUPPLIER

Your prospect's present supplier is your competitor. Don't knock him. Help your prospect do it for you. When your prospect says: "I'm satisfied with my present supplier," ask carefully planned questions that will make the prospect review the performance of his present supplier. Your competitor may be good, but he isn't perfect. Your questions may remind your prospect of some incidences of poor quality and delayed deliveries. Through this tactful method, *you* don't criticize your competitor—your prospect does.

Here are two examples of questions you can use for this purpose:

1. "Mr. Gilbert, what are your standards of quality and delivery?" The prospect's reply will be something like this: "We demand top quality and delivery as scheduled."

2. You then ask: "Are those standards being met 100 percent right now?"

The second question will probably bring to mind some problems in the past. A shipment of poor quality—parts, for example—may have caused delay and personal embarrassment.

This is the time, then, to propose a change in the present course of action—a change that will include your products and services.

This tactic is a smooth way to get the job done without openly criticizing your competitor—or the buyer's judgement. Try this idea on your next prospect who claims to be satisfied with his present supplier.

TRANSLATE GOOD FEATURES INTO BENEFITS

In Chapter 2, some examples were given of good features, such as good quality, accuracy, speed, and strength. Please review the tip "Analyze the Features of a Product" on page 20.

A very common mistake salespeople make is to limit the sales presentation to feature, feature, and feature. It is assumed that the prospect will understand the benefits he will enjoy from the good features. For example, when you say to your prospect: "This is a good quality product," you are doing only a half job of selling. Don't make that mistake. You are leaving it to the prospect to perform the most important part of the sale: You are asking him to translate that "good quality" statement into what it means to him (benefit).

What *is* a benefit? It is something of value received by the user of the product. Benefits are derived by the use of the good features. The *needs* of the purchaser are met by the good features. Here are some examples of benefits:

Protection against downtime	Prestige
Saving of money	Comfort
Saving of time	Health
Increase in profits	Security
Protection against loss	Customer satisfaction
Protection against injury	Repeat business
Longer wear	Increase in sales
Increase in production	Better taste
Reduction of costs	Peace of mind
Improvement of quality	Praise from the boss
Compliments from your friends	

In thinking of the benefits, be sure to include those that concern the individual as well as his company. Frequently, sales can be influenced by meeting the needs of the individual buyer in addition to the needs of his organization.

Let's go back to the sentence about good quality. Restructure the statement by beginning the sentence with the benefit. For example:

    You <u>will get longer wear</u> and
              (Benefit)

    <u>less downtime</u> because of the
     (Benefit)

     <u>good quality</u> of this product.
    (Good Feature)

You may have some problems in distinguishing between a feature and a benefit. The following example will clarify things for you.

Take a water glass. Pour cold, pure water into the glass. The glass now contains water that is cold and pure. All three are features. They do not provide bene-

fits until you sip the water. As you do, you receive an element that refreshes and sustains life (two benefits).

The point is that the good features lie dormant until you put them into use. Only then, after you sipped the water, did they become benefits.

Other tips in this chapter will give you additional ideas for effective feature–benefit selling.

CHART THE FEATURES AND BENEFITS OF YOUR PROPOSITION

Before making a call on a customer or prospect, it is a good idea to write down the details of the proposition you plan to sell. The very act of putting things on paper will crystallize your thinking, make you enthusiastic about your proposition, and help you express yourself clearly and concisely.

As previously stated, there is a tendency to talk endless about features, and to expect the prospect to translate those details into "what's in it for him." Giving features without stating benefits is sloppy selling.

The form shown in Figure 6–1 is a simple tool for your charting exercise. Note that the Benefit column is on the left and the Good Feature column is on the right. This arrangement sets the stage for a selling sentence. A simple "bridge" word like "because" links the benefit and good feature. Here is an example: "You will make a _____ percent profit (benefit) because of the popularity of this model (good feature)."

Before starting this charting exercise, it will be a good idea to reread the tips in Chapter 2 and the preceding tip in this chapter.

CHART THE POOR FEATURES OF YOUR PROSPECT'S PRESENT COURSE OF ACTION—AND THE LOSSES HE IS INCURRING

The charting of the poor features and losses of your prospect's present course of action helps you clarify your thinking. The review solidifies your thinking about the advan-

FIGURE 6–1 Benefits and good features chart

Your Proposition	
Write the details of your proposition to the prospect or customer. Describe what you want him to do.	
List the BENEFITS the prospect will enjoy by using the GOOD FEATURES	List the GOOD FEATURES of your proposition

tages of your proposition—and the ways it will correct the prospect's current course.

The charting of the poor features and losses of your prospect's current course of action can be a continuation of the benefit–good feature charting of *your* plan. (See Figure 6–1.)

Please refer to Figure 6–2. There is a space for describing what the prospect is now doing that you want to change. The chart then displays Poor Feature and Loss columns. This is an important tool to use as you plan your sales presentations.

The information accumulated on this chart must be used carefully. Sometimes it is wise *not* to present the information to the prospect. Instead, you may wish to use the information you've gathered to strengthen your own thinking about the benefits and good features of *your* plan.

PROGRAM YOUR BRAIN
WITH "SELLING SENTENCES"

The charting of benefits and good features sets the stage for the development of powerful "selling sentences." It is smart to program your brain with them so that they come to your lips easily and naturally.

A good selling sentence or pursuasive statement usually starts with the benefit, which is backed up by the good feature. For example:

Mr. Prospect, you will produce more pieces
<u>   </u>
                                            Benefit

at less cost because of the high speed of
   Benefit   *Good feature*

of this machine.

(Note how the word "because" links the benefit to the good feature.)

The charting of Poor Features and losses also helps to develop a "double-barreled" selling sentence. For example:

FIGURE 6–2 Poor features and losses chart

<u>The Prospect's Present Method</u>

Describe what the prospect or customer is doing <u>now</u> that you want him to change to your proposition.

List the POOR FEATURES of his present method	List the LOSSES he will suffer if he continues his present course

Mr. Prospect, you will produce more pieces
                         ‾‾‾‾‾‾‾‾‾‾‾‾‾‾‾‾‾
                               Benefit

at less cost because of the high speed of
   ‾‾‾‾‾‾‾‾‾   ‾‾‾‾‾‾‾‾‾‾
   Benefit   *Good feature*

of this machine.

If you continue to use your present, obsolete equipment

with its slower speed, you will have higher costs
    ‾‾‾‾‾‾‾‾‾‾‾‾‾‾‾‾‾   ‾‾‾‾‾‾‾‾‾‾‾
      Poor feature   *Loss*

and fail to meet your competition."
    ‾‾‾‾‾‾‾‾‾‾‾‾‾‾‾‾‾‾‾‾‾‾‾‾‾‾‾
              Loss

After charting benefits, good features, poor features, and losses, spend some time writing persuasive statements (selling sentences). Memorize them and use them in your sales presentations. You will then be able to state your case clearly, concisely, and forcefully.

CHOOSE THE RIGHT WORDS
FOR YOUR SALES PRESENTATION

Make your sales presentation concise and to the point. Choose the right words to describe your proposition: Make sure the words convey your exact meaning. They must be carefully selected for the listener—ones that he can understand, assimilate, and believe; otherwise, your time will be wasted.

Extensive research on the subject of vocabulary concluded that a broad knowledge of the exact meaning of words accompanies success. Scores of vocabulary tests are almost always in direct ratio to the person's rank in an organization. Presidents usually make better scores than vice-presidents, and vice presidents usually outscore their division heads. Throughout the various levels of a given company, the bosses tend to have larger vocabularies and better scores on vocabulary tests than their subordinates. Education has some bearing on these results, although many executives with less education scored higher on vocabulary tests than others with college degrees. It follows, then, that the development of your vocabulary will be one more asset for you as you climb the promotional ladder.

In order to improve your vocabulary, you discover words that are just beyond the boundary of your present vocabulary. You may recognize their meaning because of their proximity to words that are familiar to you, but they are not words that you use comfortably. Write these words down; look up their meanings in a dictionary and a thesaurus; practice their pronunciation; and add them to your library of words. Your vocabulary will quickly broaden—and your sales presentations will be more effective.

USE TESTIMONIALS AND SUCCESS STORIES TO SUPPORT YOUR CLAIMS

Testimonials are written proof of customer satisfaction with you, your products, and your company. They are in the form of business letters from the users of your services. They can be obtained very easily—by asking for them. Here is an example: Suppose you have just handled a delivery crisis for one of your customers and he compliments you on your service. You thank him and say, "Will you give me a letter on that?"

Two things will happen: One, you get a complimentary letter that you then show to prospects, and two, you please your customer because the act of doing you a favor has made him feel even better about you and your company.

Success stories are verbal accounts of cases where you or your fellow salespeople have provided benefits to a customer. They are exactly the same as testimonials except they are verbal. You weave success stories into your sales presentation this way: Suppose your prospect says, "I'm satisfied with my present lines. I don't need another." You respond to this by saying, "I can understand how you feel, Mr. Prospect. The dealer over in ＿＿＿＿＿ felt the same way, but I persuaded him to give me a pilot order and here is what happened . . ."

In addition to carrying copies of testimonial letters in your briefcase, put together some very powerful visual aids that will give your prospect, in just a few glances, the full impact of your array of satisfied clients. Buy some 8½" x 11" cellophane sheet protectors (the kind with black paper inserts). Take letterheads from your good clients and cut off the tops, paste them on the black sheets, and put the sheet protectors over them. This will give the prospect, in one glance, the tops of letterheads of approximately five companies (ten, if you paste on front and back). Carry these visuals in your briefcase and show them at the right moment to reinforce your claims about quality products and good service.

Your prospect rarely sees this type of visual, and it will make you stand out once more as a smooth professional.

UNDERSTAND THE DIFFERENCE BETWEEN OBJECTIONS AND "PUT-OFFS"

There is a difference between an objection and a "put-off." Both are considered a "buyer resistance," but it is a mistake to handle them in the same manner. It is important to recognize the difference between the two and employ the right tactics for each one.

As a rule, an objection is honest. That is why it is easier to handle than a put-off. There are two kinds of objections: common and specific. A *common objection* is one that is encountered by all salespeople in a given organization. For example, a company that has a product priced higher than that of its competitors will meet the objection, "Your price is too high." A *specific objection* is one that is confined to a given sales situation. For example, the prospect can't use the product because its specifications don't fit. (A good example of this is when a proposed dishwasher won't fit the space in the kitchen.)

The put-off is a much more difficult resistance to handle. This is because it is used by the prospect who is either uninterested or distracted—or doesn't understand. When you are told: "Let me think about it" or "Call me later," you are being put off. You have not gained the attention you need, and you have not created the desire to hear more. Then you know that there is something wrong with your presentation.

Busy prospects develop defense mechanisms to save their time. They have assembled a storehouse of tested put-offs, and they use them freely on those salespeople who don't capture their attention and create interest.

Understand what is happening to you at the put-off. Then review your presentation: Check your visual aids, develop better probing questions and selling sentences. The put-offs will decrease in direct ratio to the improvement of your presentation.

SUGGESTIONS FOR THE REBUTTAL OF OBJECTIONS

First, let us define "rebut." According to Webster's dictionary, rebut means to answer the arguments of an opponent in debate. In a sales situation, the prospect is *not* an opponent and should not be treated as such. In a sales interview, the rebut is the salesperson's reply to the prospect's objection to a point in the proposition being offered. The rebut, in this context, is a calm, reasoned reply to the prospect. Here are some guidelines for handling (or rebutting) the objection:

1. Restate before you rebut.
2. Inquire before you rebut.
3. Concede before you rebut.
4. Replace the prospect's "Yes—but" with "Yes—and."
5. Stop rebutting when you have made your point.
6. Rebut only what you need to rebut.

By *restating before you rebut*, you (1) give yourself some time to collect your thoughts, and (2) please your prospect by this evidence that you understand his objection.

By *asking questions before you rebut*, you draw out from the prospect more pertinent information that clarifies his objection and pinpoints the specific area of difference.

By *conceding before you rebut,* you please your prospect and soften him for your rebuttal. Concede, in this case, does not mean agreement with your prospect's objection. Instead, it simply means that you understand the prospect's position. For example, you can say: "I can understand why you feel about this as you do—we *did* have some problems with that product some time ago and we have learned a lot from that experience." This is a concession before you proceed with your rebuttal.

"Yes—but" is a common opening to a rebuttal and frequently triggers additional arguments. Use "Yes—and" as a more effective opener. Here is an example: "Yes, Mr. James, *and* we soon learned how to handle that problem and this is what we did . . ." Stop rebutting as soon as you have made your point and go on with your presentation. Don't make a big deal out of it.

Rebut only what you need to rebut, and that means only the prospect's key objection as pinpointed by the questions you asked.

USE THE RIGHT DEGREE OF AGGRESSIVENESS FOR EACH CALL

Only *you* can measure the right amount of aggressiveness to get the desired action from your prospect. Aggressiveness can be overdone or underdone: A lot depends on you and your approach. And also, much depends on the person you are trying to sell.

You may not be "built" for tough, hard-closing techniques. They may be foreign to your breeding and background. If you are uncomfortable with that type of selling, don't use it. It will do you more harm than good. Your inner feelings of self-dissatisfaction and uncertainty will surface during your presentation. They will be made evident by some of the following signals:

- An abrasive and argumentative attitude.
- A persistent pursuit of a point or suggestion that is of secondary importance to the prospect.

- Your body language indicating fear, uncertainty, or anxiety.
- An artifical and tense presentation that belies the benefits and good features you are offering.

Your choice to use this overaggressive approach may be instigated by an overaggressive manager. Your manager may not realize that other types of selling may be more productive—at least for you.

Being persistent but not obnoxious is a technique that takes much thought and practice. *All* salespeople must be persistent, and that persistence must be tempered by plain social tact that helps determine the amount of "push" needed in each phase of a sales situation.

Good salesmanship includes social interaction. It requires a constant awareness of the other person's reactions to you, your product, your statements, and your questions. It takes practice and concentration to be skilled in social interaction. When you concentrate on the other person, you get an instant reaction—either positive or negative—to your sales techniques. Your expertise, then, in social interaction will help you to determine when to be aggressive and when to "shift gears" and adopt a softer course of action with that particular prospect.

Do what comes naturally to you and your special makeup. Make sure that you are offering a good product that will exactly fill the needs of that particular prospect—one in which he will profit more from the purchase than you will from the sale. Then make your presentation in a positive and enthusiastic manner—and in a tone that is right for both you and your prospect.

RESTATE THE KEY POINTS OF YOUR PROPOSAL BEFORE ASKING FOR THE ORDER

Sum up the salient features of your proposition before you try for the close. This is a good way to make sure your prospect *thoroughly* understands what you want him to do. If you don't summarize—and he doesn't completely understand—then you will get a put-off or a turn-down.

When you call on a prospect, your brain is crystal clear on the reasons why the prospect should buy your product; *his* brain, on the other hand, is filled with many details, and few of them pertain to you or your product. Also, he may have had some telephone calls and distractions during your session with him. It is not surprising that after fifty or sixty minutes of your presentation and his distractions, he may be confused. If you ask for the decision before you clear up that confusion, you are almost certain to fail. So, form the habit of briefly reviewing your proposition before asking him to buy.

Here is a format for a quick, concise summary:

1. In three or four sentences, tell your prospect *what* you want him to do.
2. Then tell him, in "selling sentences," *why* he should do it—and what's in it for him.
3. Tactfully review his present course of action—the one that you want him to change in favor of yours.
4. State the price of your product or service.
5. Quickly follow that up with the return on investment he will enjoy.
6. Ask for the order.

To repeat, the summary is important at the close. Plan to use it in your sales presentations. A concise sum-up will significantly reduce the number of put-offs and turn-downs you receive.

ASK FOR THE ORDER
BY ASKING A CLOSING QUESTION

The "close," of course, is the culmination of the whole act of selling. It is the payoff for all the work and planning you have done so far.

The close isn't necessarily obtaining an order for your product. Other closes might be to gain agreement for a survey, or permission to make a demonstration, or acceptance of your invitation to visit corporate headquarters.

Every contact you make with your prospect or customer should have an objective. When you gain that objective, you have obtained the action desired for that particular contact; that is, a close for that call.

The way to ask for the action desired is to ask a closing question. Do not make a statement—ask a question. That question should be followed by silence. You force the prospect to break the silence and make the decision. At this point, body language is also important. Good eye contact and an alert posture, for example, will signal to the prospect that this is the time for a decision.

Practice good closing questions so that your memory bank is abundantly supplied with a good selection to be used as each sales situation requires. Good closing questions should be open-ended. A closed question could result in a flat "No."

Open-ended questions that start with Where, When, Who, What and How will help you get that favorable decision. Here are some examples:

"*Where* shall we deliver it?"

"*When* may we make delivery?"

"*Who* shall we call when it is ready?"

"*What* is the best time for instructing your people?"

"*How* do you want to handle payment?"

Determine the objective for each call. Then program your brain with closing questions that will gain that objective—the close.

ASK FOR THE PURCHASE ORDER NUMBER —NOT THE PURCHASE ORDER

As soon as you get a purchase order number, you can ship and bill immediately; if you ask only for the purchase order *form*, you face a one- to two-week delay. Anything can happen in that period: The customer may change his mind, or for other reasons, cancel the order.

A purchase order number can be obtained in minutes. The prospect can telephone his purchasing department and have a number assigned to him. It is followed up by a purchase order requisition from which the purchase order form (with that number) is finally typed.

When you get the p.o. number, you've got the order and you can move quickly to clinch it by fast shipping and billing. At your next close, ask: "Do I need a purchase order number?" The prospect will reply in one of three ways:

"Yes, you do."

"No, you don't."

"I'm not ready to buy."

When you get either of the first two answers, you've got the order. It's a quick, casual way to get a decision.

DON'T TRY TO SELL
TOO MANY ITEMS (OR IDEAS)
DURING ONE INTERVIEW

There is often a tendency for a salesperson to try to sell too many products during a single sales call—in order to get the most "mileage" out of every sales minute. If you do this, it can cause some problems. It can create a decision conflict between one item and another in your product line. For example, if your prospect has only so much to spend, he can hesitate about favoring one product at the expense of another. It can cause an "I'll have to think it over" put-off.

Try to determine your prospect's needs in terms of his priorities, and decide which of your products will fill his most important need. Then concentrate on the sale of that product during one sales call. After that sale is safely consummated, you can then concentrate on the other needs. Do this again and again in terms of your prospect's priorities.

By giving your prospect too many things to think about you risk "muddying up the water." Take first things first and avoid those time-wasting put-offs that are caused by decision conflicts.

A SALE "PSYCHS YOU UP"
—THAT'S THE TIME
TO MAKE ANOTHER, AND ANOTHER

Your attitude is extremely important for effective selling. Take full advantage of your good attitudes. When you are "high," play it for all it's worth. That's the best time to sell again and again. It starts a winning streak: One win charges you up for another, and another.

In selling, the highs are started by those wonderful words "I'll take it," or "I'll write a purchase order," or "You've got the order." Those words are thrilling even to the most sophisticated salesperson.

An agreement to buy is a sure sign of product satisfaction. Certainly, your prospect would not buy your proposition unless he saw the benefits to him and his company—hence, the okay. Probably of greater importance to you is the self-satisfaction gained by that purchase. It is also proof that you have done a good job of selling and that the buyer approves of you as well as your product.

As you walk out with that order, you are on "cloud nine." You are all psyched up. You have a tremendous sense of well-being, and you are proud of your company, your product—and yourself. That is the optimum time to start another sale. You have that precious power of enthusiasm that is so contagious. Call on another prospect, and another, and another. You will start a winning streak—which pays handsome commissions.

TREAT THE SECRETARY
AS THE PROSPECT'S "ADMINISTRATIVE
ASSISTANT"

The secretary can be an ally or an obstacle. Treat her right and she will help you.

Your job is to sell yourself as well as your company and its products. The secretary's job is to shield her boss against unnecessary interruptions. But *that* assignment has another side to it. The secretary (the administrative assistant kind) is also on the alert for ideas, products, and services that will help her boss. She can be sold on necessary interruptions—if you give her a chance.

Give her information about you, your company, your product, how others have benefited from your services, and the reasons why her boss should grant you some time. Also, give her an idea of how much time you will need.

Treat the administrative assistant with the respect and dignity she deserves. She can be the one who opens the door for you to the sale—and to years of repeat business. (Everything suggested here also applies to other staff members. They can be of great help to you, too.

A SERVICE CONTRACT
CAN BE A SALES ASSET

Many companies' products require service. This, in turn, requires trained service personnel. A high-caliber repairman operating in your territory can be an important goodwill ambassador for you. This is especially true when you have a service contract arrangement with your customers.

Service contracts call for regularly scheduled inspections of your customers' equipment. Thus, a well-trained service representative can supplement your sales calls and give your company additional representation—and the added coverage is paid for by the customer through the terms of the service contract.

Many companies recognize the powerful advantage of this sales–service combination. In addition to service training, their repairmen are taught the techniques of good customer relations—which is a form of salesmanship.

If your company offers repair service, you will be wise to work closely with the service personnel. Help support the service contract plan. Compare notes with the service people who call on your accounts, when encouraged to do so, they can alert you to trends and activities. This additional information and support will strengthen your sales efforts with those accounts.

A sales–service team can provide that "one-two punch" that is so vital to the maintenance of profitable repeat business.

Tips on
the Face-to-Face
Sales Call

The face-to-face sales call is the most common, and usually the most productive, of the four types of contact made by a salesperson.

Once again, the tips presented in this and other chapters pertain to calls on customers as well as prospects. This point is reemphasized because it is so easy to take customers for granted—to handle them carelessly and casually.

Stand Out!

The tips that follow are designed to help you stand out in your work with both prospects and customers. You need that winning edge in *all* contacts.

In some respects, the face-to-face sales call is easier to make than contacts by mail, telephone, and written proposal. For example, when you are with the account, it is easier to gain favorable attention and *hold* it. Also, when you can observe the conditions under which the prospect is working, you can "shift gears" to cope with adverse situations.

Conversely, when the prospect can observe *you*, you must be prepared to be inspected for appearance, behavior, and professionalism. You are "on stage"—and put yourself in a very vulnerable position if you have been careless in your dress, grooming, and the handling of your sales tools.

The number of face-to-face interviews are far to few. Even the best salespeople will have difficulty in averaging over six appointment calls per day. That is probably fewer than 900 minutes in a given week to be face-to-face with your accounts. That is only 38 percent of the maximum contact time a salesperson could have.

Under those circumstances, you've got to be good (effective). This is why every possible technique is important for consideration and acceptance. Once a technique is tested and proven effective it should be practiced—and then integrated into your own pattern of salesmanship.

With those odds, you can't leave anything to chance. Therefore, add the following tips to those suggested by your company. Use them as your own "gut feeling" dictates. When you know about them—and have weighed their merits—you are in an excellent position to use them at the proper time, and to your advantage

PLAN YOUR SALES CALL
AND CARRY YOUR CALL PLANNER SHEET
WITH YOU AS A PROMPTER

Every sales call should be carefully planned. It is easy to become careless—especially when you call repeatedly on the same customer. Professional salesmanship includes: planning, preparation, execution, and evaluation for every important call.

Every call must have a definite objective. Make sure you know, in very definite terms, what you hope to accomplish on each call that you make. Also, for planning purposes, dissect the average call into five segments to:

- Gain favorable attention.
- Develop a dialogue with the prospect.
- Make the proposal stating the benefits and good features of your service and product.
- Be prepared to handle all possible objections.
- Ask for the desired action.

The actual call may not proceed in this order, but it is important to examine each phase and be prepared to handle each one.

Your plans may be condensed on a plain piece of notepaper or they can be written on a form similar to The Sales Call Planner Sheet shown in Figure 7–1. It doesn't really matter how you do it as long as you *do* do it. In the pressure of the day's sales calls, it is so easy to become "ho-hum" on each call. Accurate planning and disciplined follow-through is what separates the real pros from the mediocre salespeople.

In the entertainment field, experienced platform experts such as Bob Hope and Danny Thomas never appear on stage without a careful array of prompter cards, which they refer to as needed to keep them on track. In a similar manner, you should use The Sales Call Planner Sheet. Fill the sheet out for each important call and carry it with you in your coat pocket. Then, as you wait for your prospect, refer to it so that your opening remarks, your probing questions, your benefit–feature statement in the form of selling sentences, your replies to objections, and your closing questions are all presented as you had planned.

The planned presentation (not a "canned sales pitch") is the mark of the true professional. It will make you stand out, and your hard preparatory work will pay off.

PLAN AND PRACTICE
THE DEMONSTRATION OF YOUR PRODUCT

The demonstration is the physical action taken to prove the claims in your proposal. It is also sometimes used to overcome an objection by proving that the objection is not valid. The demonstration has enormous psychological value,

FIGURE 7-1 Sales call planner

1. Company _____

2. Person/persons to be called on

   _____ Title _____

   _____ Title _____

3. Background experiences _____

   _____

4. Objectives of this call _____

   _____

5. Strategies for handling the interview

   (a) Gaining favorable attention _____

   _____

   (b) Probing for the prospect's problems and principal interests

   _____

   (c) The proposition in terms of Good Features and Benefits

   _____

   _____

   _____

   Objections to anticipate _____

   _____

   Planned answers to those objections _____

   _____

   (d) Closing techniques to be used to get the action desired

   _____

   _____

6. Sales tools and materials to take on this call _____

   _____

   _____

especially when it gets the prospect "into the act" as a participant in the proceedings.

A word of warning: In demonstrating the product, there is a common tendency to confine the whole verbal explanation to "nuts and bolts." Don't expect the prospect to convert your technical descriptions to *benefits*—to "what's in it for him." During the demonstration, you have an excellent opportunity to use selling sentences—in which you give the benefit *because* of the physical features. Here again is where your "programmed" brain will tell you *how* to say it as you do your demonstrating.

Like so many other things you do in sales work, the demonstration must be planned and practiced. *Practice your sales presentation before a mirror. Practice* handling the product smoothly and expertly, and *practice* your verbal presentation timed with your physical actions. Use a cassette player to capture your sales talk. Play it back to check your enunciation, delivery, and vocabulary.

Do it again and again until you have it perfect. The demonstration step is frequently near to the closing step. Make sure that perfect demonstration leads to that close.

COORDINATE THE USE OF YOUR SALES TOOLS WITH YOUR VERBAL PRESENTATION

It is so easy to overlook some of the many props available in the daily job of selling. Sales tools are the things you can use and show to make a smooth, powerful presentation.

A salesperson with the right tools, and the practice that makes them come to life in his hands, is an inspiring sight to watch in action. He is like a professional actor stepping onto a Broadway stage—confident, smooth, and practiced in every word and gesture.

A salesperson has many tools at his command. Every one of them, when properly used, will help him make more sales. Many tools are such obvious, everyday items that they are frequently overlooked or used sloppily. But they can be very helpful, even vital, when combined with other tools and used in support of a verbal presentation.

Here is a list of some of the many sales tools:

Briefcase	Testimonials
Calling card	Demonstrator
Price book	Order pad
Sales brochures	Appointment book
Charts and other visuals	

When a salesperson plans and practices the use of sales tools, it becomes a habit, leaving his mind free to adapt to new situations as they arise.

Through the eyes of the buyer, the practiced salesperson is impressive and assuring because he looks and acts as if he knows what he is doing and why he is doing it. The busy prospect is entitled to every communication tool that will convey to him the complete sales story in a smooth, concise, dramatic manner. With this type of presentation, the buyer is thus impelled to respond in a positive fashion.

It all takes practice (preferably before a mirror and with a cassette player). This investment of time and effort will pay enormous dividends—and make it even more fun being a professional.

TAKE ADVANTAGE OF VISUAL AIDS

Selling is a form of teaching. You want the prospect to learn about your products and their benefits to him. Many studies have been made on the learning process. We know that we learn:

6 percent through taste, touch, and smell
11 percent through hearing
83 percent through sight

Professional teachers make good use of these percentages. They employ blackboards, flipcharts, overhead projectors, films, cassettes, and computers to help their pupils learn by sight and sound.

But, after your prospect learns about your product and its benefits, you want him to retain that information—and do something about it.

Additional studies on retention show that we remember:

    10 percent of what we read
    20 percent of what we hear
    30 percent of what we see
    50 percent *of what we see and hear*

It is obvious, therefore, that the best way to help your prospect to *learn* and *remember* is to support your verbal presentation with visual aids. They can be simple structures such as diagrams, charts, and pictures of the product.

Some companies provide their salespeople with audiovisual presentations. They assure the company that its sales representatives tell the sales story the way the company wants it told. A slide/tape presentation, for example, does meet the standards for learning and remembering, and in many cases is quite effective.

On the other hand, audiovisual presentations require a more formal setting that many salespeople find uncomfortable. Also, a particular sales situation may not require the full story as it is given in a fixed presentation. In most cases, salespeople devise their own visual aid kits. There is nothing wrong with that as long as those visual aids are effective.

One of the most common visual aid kits is the ring binder that contains photographs, diagrams, and charts. It can be used under adverse conditions such as a lobby interview or across a cluttered desk. Some presentation binders contain pages with pockets. The pockets can be loaded with material that is especially pertinent to a specific prospect. Thus, the binder can be specially loaded and cocked for each sales call.

The use of visual aids must be coordinated with your sales talk. If you are clumsy in handling your props, they will cause more harm than good. Coordination of the visual aids with your sales talk must be practiced. For example, you must know each page of a binder so well that you can turn to it without fumbling, point to key parts of the visual from the side or top, and give your verbal presentation as the prospect looks at the pertinent visual. That takes confidence, and practice breeds confidence.

Selling without the use of visuals is difficult. Selling with visual aids will improve the learning process—and make your presentations much more effective. Use your ingenuity. Keep asking yourself:

How can I present my sales story more effectively to the busy buyer?

What visual aids can I devise that will capture and hold his attention?

What visuals will help him learn and retain my message?

Study the methods of others. For example, pay attention to T.V. commercials. Those advertisers spend tremendous sums for sixty seconds on T.V. Watch how they use visual aids to reinforce their "pitches."

Your planning and preparation of visual aids is a challenge. Your practice with them—and their use in your sales interviews—will significantly increase your sales productivity.

USE YOUR SALES BROCHURES AS SALES AIDS —BUT RETAIN CONTROL OF THEM

There are two ways to use your sales brochure: as a mailing or "leave behind" piece; or as a visual aid during the sales interview.

The first method is the most common. You mail the sales brochure to generate initial interest prior to the sales call—or you leave the brochure with the prospect upon the completion of the call.

The second method is one that is frequently bungled by some representatives. They employ the brochure as a visual aid. It is used to reinforce a verbal description of an important product feature. This is where they can lose control of the interview. If they hand the sales brochure to the prospect, they switch the prospect's attention from what they are saying to what the brochure is showing.

Don't make that mistake. Retain possession of your sales brochure. Use it as you would a chart or other visual aid. Hold it up for good visibility. Point to those key features. Describe them. Coordinate your verbal description with your finger pointing and hand gestures. To do this takes practice and concentration. You must know your brochure so well that you can point and describe as you view it from the side or top.

The brochure can be a powerful sales tool if you retain control of it during the interview. When it is mishandled, it can cause you to bungle the sales call and possibly lose the sale.

RECOGNIZE THE DIFFERENCE
BETWEEN THE "COLD" CALL
AND THE APPOINTMENT CALL

The cold call (sometimes called "cold canvass call") is different from the appointment call. It is so named because you call on the prospect without warning. You enter his premises without invitation and with few facts about him or his company. You ask him (through the receptionist) to stop what he is doing and interrupt his schedule.

Picture the prospect at his desk. He has the day well planned. He is busy on one of the scheduled tasks. His phone rings. It is the receptionist who announces your presence in the lobby. His first reaction is one of cold indifference to your call. But perhaps company policy demands courtesy to all salespeople, so he is required to see you. He either sends for you or goes to the lobby to meet with you.

Under these "cold" conditions, you must be especially good. You must be prepared to gain favorable attention under adverse circumstances.

The appointment call is vastly different from the cold call. Advance planning has been done by both you and your prospect. The prospect has set aside some time for you. You have done some research so you know something about the prospect and some possible problems. At the appointed time, you meet under favorable conditions.

The usual purpose of a cold call is to make the initial contact, learn about the company, its products and its people, and, in general, get "the lay of the land." The usual objective of the appointment call is to make the sale or to start positive steps toward it. There is a place in your daily schedule for both cold calls and appointment calls.

Build a "framework" of appointments for each sales day. Don't schedule the appointments too close together. Allow some extra time for an unexpected delay—or for a longer interview. Then, when time permits, fill in the extra time with cold calls. Make them on your way to the next appointment call.

A good mix of cold calls and appointment calls will "charge you up." Both are challenging—and the challenges will keep you alert and on your toes.

BE PREPARED FOR THE "LOBBY INTERVIEW"

The interview in the prospect's lobby occurs most frequently on the cold call rather than the appointment call. It sometimes catches the salesperson unprepared for it, which is one of the reasons he or she might avoid future cold calls.

The prospect frequently chooses the lobby interview to save his time. In the lobby, *he* has the advantage. He can act hurried, glance at his watch, and use a tested put-off at the first opportunity. It is an easy way to "brush off" the salesperson and still satisfy the company rules concerning courtesies to salespeople. In many lobby interviews, the prospect remains standing, thus making it even more difficult for the salesperson.

Be prepared for that lobby interview. Plan and practice a brief—but strong—presentation. The purpose of the call is to create initial interest, gain information, and set the stage for an appointment call.

Develop a binder or folder specifically designed for the lobby interview. Have it contain visual aids that can be used as you stand with the prospect. Such a special sales tool, quickly removed from your briefcase, will help you get the job done smoothly and professionally. Plan some "leave behind" literature. Have a notepad ready.

Your careful preparation and practice for the lobby interview are the keys to a polished performance. And that impressive performance, in turn, will set the stage for a profitable relationship with your new prospect.

PRACTICE "CREATIVE IMAGERY" ON YOUR WAY TO THE CALL

"Creative imagery" is picturing the events of the call as you expect them to happen. It is a tactic for psyching oneself up for the face-to-face interview. And it is a method for the last-minute review of opening remarks, sales tools to be used, and objections to be handled.

As you approach the prospect's office, turn off the car radio and concentrate. Picture yourself doing the following:

- Checking your briefcase
- Leaving the car
- Entering the prospect's place of business
- Greeting people along the way (calling them by name—if known)
- Meeting the prospect
- Making your opening remarks
- Developing a dialogue
- Making your proposal
- Handling your sales tools
- Meeting objections
- Asking for the desired action
- Departing

You will discover that this method of "imagining" will help you make a smooth, enthusiastic, and professional presentation.

Try it! It works!

LOAD AND COCK YOUR BRIEFCASE
FOR EACH CALL

Carry a stand-up type of briefcase (not an attaché case). Use the briefcase as a portable filing cabinet and load it for each sales call. Place your visuals, brochures, and other sales tools in the order of their anticipated use during the sales presentation.

The briefcase is one of your most important sales tools. When used properly, it can enhance your smooth sales presentation. It is as important to the salesperson as an M16 rifle is to an infantryman. It should be loaded and cocked for each sales call. This takes planning and preparation for each call. It also takes practice—practice before a mirror—so that you can reach into your briefcase without fumbling and extract that special sales tool that is pertinent to your verbal presentation. Your physical movements should be timed with your oral explanation. Timing is as important to the salesperson as to the professional actor on stage. Remember, there are only 2082 "contact hours" in the whole year—and very few of those hours are spent in direct contact with the prospect or customer. That is why the time you *do* have with the buyer is precious and should be used to full advantage. This takes practice, practice, and more practice.

We suggest the stand-up type of briefcase rather than the attaché case because with an attache' case you can do three things—*and all three are wrong*. One is to put it on the prospect's desk: This is taboo. The second is to place it on the floor and then try to maintain a dignified presentation as you reach down to remove objects from the case. The third way is to place it on your lap: When you raise the cover, you create a barrier between you and the prospect.

The free-standing briefcase, used as a portable filing cabinet and loaded and "cocked" for each call, is far better than the attaché case. It is one more tool to help you look good in the eyes of the prospect. (See Figure 7–2.)

BEAT THAT "FREEZE"

The "freeze" happens to every salesperson sometime in his or her career. It stops you from opening that prospect's door,

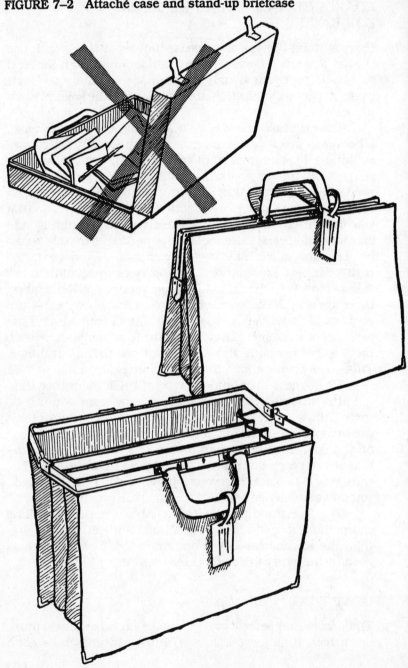

FIGURE 7–2 Attaché case and stand-up briefcase

and usually occurs when you are making "cold canvass" calls. You are uneasy about walking into new surroundings and meeting new people; you are afraid of rebuff and embarrassment, and you feel like an intruder—like an unwanted peddler.

As you hesitate in that crucial moment—and at that psychological barrier—you have reached an important point in your career. Only *you* can handle the problem.

First, analyze the reasons for the "freeze." What is making you stop—and perhaps turn away? The most obvious reasons have already been suggested. But the *real* reasons are deeper—and not so obvious. You will never be a top performer until you dig out those reasons and truly understand them.

The first step in handling the "freeze" problem is to recognize rationalization for what it is—an enemy to any potential top performer. It is easy under these circumstances to rationalize that the prospect is probably too busy to see you; he won't like to be disturbed; it is too close to the lunch hour; or you don't have the materials you need.

The "freeze" and the turning away are relatively unimportant—it is the harm they cause that is important. When you give in to that "freeze," you can start a chain reaction and become "gun-shy" to all similar encounters. It can create a serious, long-range problem.

Therefore, beat that "freeze." Pause outside the prospect's door for two or three minutes. Ponder the situation. What's happening to you? *Are* you a peddler? *Are* you a nuisance? What *do* you have to offer? Why *should* this prospect see you? What's in it for him—and his company? What have you done for other companies in a similar type of business? How did *they* profit from your services? What testimonials and success stories do you have that will attract his favorable attention?

The positive answers to these questions will improve your attitude. You realize that if you do it right, this call can be the start of a relationship that will be bilateral: It will be so mutually beneficial that the prospect will thank you for entering that door. (Note: If you don't get positive answers to your self-questioning, then don't make the call. You are wasting his time and yours. Do some research. Compile testimonials and success stories. They will give you the sales ammunition you need. And they will psych you up so that you can't wait to open that door.)

PLAN THE EFFECTIVE USE
OF YOUR CALLING CARD

The calling card can be an effective sales tool when handled properly. Unfortunately, it is frequently mishandled—and used as an afterthought. The proper use of the calling card is part of that ensemble of professionalism. It can help you stand out.

Use your calling card as a visual aid to support your verbal introduction of yourself and your company. You make it easy for the other person when the initial greeting is done smoothly and professionally.

Before entering your prospect's office, take three calling cards from your card case. Have them handy to avoid fumbling. For salesmen, it is a good idea to place them in the left-hand coat pocket; for sales*women*, place them in your bag or briefcase for easy retrieval.

The three cards are for the receptionist, the secretary, and the prospect. You may not need all three. The point is that when they are in easy reach, you avoid awkward fumbling.

DON'T SIT DOWN
IN THE PROSPECT'S LOBBY
OR RECEPTION AREA

Remain standing after introducing yourself to the receptionist. There are two reasons for this tactic: You will get faster action; and you remain "charged up" and ready to do business.

When salespeople are comfortably seated, the receptionist is relaxed, and little effort is made to speed things up. But if you remain standing, the receptionist will become uncomfortable. Soon she will remind the prospect that you are waiting. But don't be obnoxious. Just be calm about it. Review your notes and act businesslike. It will bring results.

The second reason to remain standing is psychological. Chances are you are all "psyched up" when you enter the lobby. The longer you wait, the "flatter" you get. This is especially true when you are seated along with others who are patiently waiting. When you remain standing, you look different, act different, and feel different. It will pay dividends when you face your prospect.

BE ALERT TO THE VARIOUS SEATING ARRANGEMENTS IN THE PROSPECT'S OFFICE

There are advantages and disadvantages to the various seating arrangements in the average prospect's office. It is important to know about them—and take advantage of them when possible. Even when you have no choice, it is smart to know what you are up against—and do something about it— if you can.

The typical position of the chair for the salesperson is directly in front of the prospect's desk. This is probably the way the prospect planned it—and wants it. When you are directed to that seat, you must go along with it. You have no choice. Chances are the desk is cluttered with objects: *Do not move any of them.* You must make your presentation despite those obstacles. When you know you might be put in that position, plan your presentation accordingly. Use visual aids that will bridge the cluttered desk.

The area behind the prospect's desk is the prospect's psychological "comfort zone." Do not invade that area. Do not go behind the prospect's desk for any reason. Such a move will create a conscious or subconscious resistance to you.

Some offices are furnished with a davenport or settee. It is usually lower (in height) to the prospect's chair. If possible, avoid it. It puts you at a disadvantage.

In many large offices you will sometimes find a separate conference area away from the prospect's desk. It is usually an arrangement comprised of a small table surrounded by several chairs. This permits a more informal discussion, which is to the advantage of both the seller and the buyer.

When you are a "guest" of the prospect, you are expected to follow his seating directions. When you know what to expect, plan to cope with those conditions that are beyond your control.

DON'T SMOKE
WHILE YOU ARE WITH YOUR PROSPECT

Avoid smoking when you are working with your prospect. He may "light up" and offer you a cigarette—or he may be a nonsmoker. In either case, don't smoke during the sales interview.

There is a good reason for this suggestion. When you are making a sales presentation, you want 100 percent (or as much as possible) of the prospect's attention. You hold that attention through good eye contact, visual aids, probing questions, and an interesting verbal explanation.

You create problems for yourself when you smoke and use an ashtray. You distract the prospect's attention. His eyes will follow your hands as you flick the ashes. He may move the ashtray for your convenience. The whole business creates an unnecessary distraction—just when you need every advantage you can get.

Refrain from smoking during the sales call. Gaining the maximum attention of the prospect will make it all worthwhile.

DON'T DRINK COFFEE
WHILE MAKING YOUR SALES PRESENTATION

This tip is similar to the preceding one on smoking—for the same reasons. There are too many unnecessary distractions when sipping coffee. The prospect searches for a coaster; he nervously watches to see that your cup is not going to spill; and his eyes follow your cup as you lift it to your lips. That makes the selling process more difficult, and it isn't worth it.

When offered a cup of coffee, simply say, "No, thank you. I've just had some." The prospect may be secretly relieved by your refusal. There is another reason for refusing coffee. In most cases, the secretary is asked to get it for you. That creates additional distractions and questions.

In addition, the secretary may secretly resent being treated like a servant. So why create *that* problem for yourself?

SOME MISCELLANEOUS "DOS AND DON'TS" FOR A SALES CALL

Follow the Rules When Parking

Almost all companies have a parking space reserved for visitors. Look for it—and use it! Don't park in a reserved space. It may belong to the person you are trying to sell. Taking his parking space is a sure way to ruin the sale.

Don't Use the Company Telephone Without Permission

If you have to make a telephone call while waiting in the lobby, use a public phone if one is available. Don't use the company phone except for an emergency—and then make the call as brief as possible.

While you are with your prospect, you may have to call your office to verify something that is pertinent to that interview. That is the *only* reason for such a call. In consideration of the prospect's time, make that call as brief as possible.

Leave Your Outer Coat in the Lobby

Remove your raincoat, topcoat, or overcoat and leave it in the prospect's lobby. There is almost always a hanging closet or space available. Do the same with rubbers and overshoes.

You look uncomfortable when wearing an outer coat in the prospect's office, and that is one more unnecessary distraction. Avoid it! In addition, a wet coat may leave marks on the furniture—and *that* won't please the prospect.

You are "on stage" at all times while you are on the prospect's premises—even as you leave. Make your departure as soon as the interview is over. Quit while you are ahead. Thank the prospect for his time and thank the secretary for her help. Say good-bye to the receptionist (and call her by name) as you pass through the lobby.

These little courtesies and considerations all add up in your favor. They help you pave the way for return calls and friendly receptions.

USE PAUSE AND SILENCE TO DRAMATIZE YOUR PRESENTATION

One of the marks of the experienced, confident salesperson is his or her effective use of pause and silence during the sales interview. Conversely, one of the signs of a nervous, uncertain salesperson is the hurried monologue and the torrent of words. It takes courage to use pause and silence—but their effects are powerful.

Try the pause on your next call. Use it in combination with body language to signify thoughtful consideration of a point. By pausing before responding to a prospect's remark or question, you indicate to him the importance of his comment.

Try using silence at the close of the sales interview. Sum up your proposition, ask a closing question, maintain good eye contact—and then remain silent. This is called "the silent close." Wait for your prospect to break that silence.

Plan pauses and silences in your sales presentations. They are effective—and they will make you look good to the prospect.

HOW TO SELL TO A COMMITTEE

Many products and installations require group decisions for the purchases. A "big ticket sale" is seldom made to a single decision maker. Even a small sale requires more than one approval when several departments are involved in the use of the product. This means that the salesperson must be prepared to make a presentation to a buying committee—usually a group of executives. Such a presentation is a form of public speaking. Some salespeople, accustomed to dealing only on a one-on-one basis with the prospect, are very uncomfortable when addressing a group and experience stage fright.

Making a presentation to a group ("group selling") takes even more thought than making a presentation to a single prospect. There are two basic problems: stage fright; and the fact that each person in the group must be sold on the merits of the proposition in terms of his special interests. Your solutions to both problems are planning, preparation and practice.

Problem #1:
Stage Fright

Nervousness in public speaking is natural. You *should* be nervous, but it must be *controlled* nervousness. (The coaches of athletes *want* the athletes to be nervous—to have "butterflies." It is the controlled nervousness that makes them champions.) The control comes from planning, preparation, and practice. When you know that you have planned well, prepared thoroughly, and practiced faithfully, you are ready and eager to go "on stage."

Problem #2:
Selling Each Person in the Group

Plan your presentation as follows.

1. Think of the special interests of each member of the group. Know his name, rank, responsibility, and problems. Plan your presentation to include the special, individual interests.
2. Be crystal clear in your own mind of the purpose of your presentation. Review your written, formal proposal. (Distribute copies *after* you make your presentation.)
3. Write your opening, body, and close.

4. Leave time after your presentation for questions and answers. (In a large meeting, repeat the question before answering it.)

5. Develop visual aids to reinforce your verbal presentation. (Make sure they are large enough to be visible to all.) Practice with them. Coordinate their use with your verbal presentation.

6. From your written presentation, make notes on 4" x 6" cards. Use them as prompters during your practice and actual presentation.

7. Have a rough "seating chart" ready. With the aid of your prospect, fill in the names when the participants are seated. Refer to the chart (if needed) to call a person *by name* when referring to a point of special interest to him.

Group selling requires a high degree of professionalism. You will be effective when you plan, prepare, and practice.

KEEP YOUR CAR NEAT AND CLEAN
TO MAINTAIN THAT GOOD IMPRESSION

There is an old saying: "A man is judged by the company he keeps." So also a person is judged by the car he or she keeps, and this is particularly true for salespeople.

You can't predict when you might have a guest in your car. Your prospect may suddenly ask for a ride—or walk with you out to the parking lot. Have your car "ready for inspection" at all times. A sloppy car (littered with children's toys, ashtrays filled with cigarette stubs, muddy floor mats, and dirty windows) can undo all your hard work to develop that professional image.

Keep your car clean by frequent washes. "Drive-thru" car washes are relatively inexpensive. Give your car's interior a daily inspection, making it as thorough and as critical as your inspection of your clothing and your personal grooming. It will help to maintain that "ensemble of professionalism" that is so vital to successful selling.

DON'T OVERDO THE ENTERTAINMENT
OF CUSTOMERS AND PROSPECTS

It is easy to get carried away with the entertainment of accounts. The purpose of wining and dining, of course, is to get and/or maintain business. It is easy to rationalize that lunches, dinners, and drinks are all part of the "art of salesmanship."

Within reasonable limits, quiet, dignified lunches with business associates *are* good tactical devices for building rapport and determining their needs and objectives. But it is easy to let it all get out of control.

When you have done a good job of consultative selling, you have developed a proposition that is mutually beneficial to the buyer as well as the seller. You are offering a bilateral contract. It is therefore unnecessary to *buy* your sale with excessive entertainment.

Many professional purchasing agents believe very strongly in the "bilateral contract" concept. They know that consultative salespeople can offer powerful assistance to their objectives of profitable buying. Therefore, in regular luncheon sessions with respected salespeople, they frequently insist on paying their share of the meal tabs.

It takes good judgment to determine just how far to go in the entertainment of customers and prospects. Generally speaking, it is better to do too little rather than too much. Quality salesmanship will do more good for your account—and for yourself.

Tips on Telephone Techniques

Telephoning is one of the four methods of contacting customers and prospects. There are a number of good reasons for using the telephone, such as the following:

- Maintaining the sales momentum between sales calls
- Delivering information
- Obtaining information
- Making appointments
- Selling ideas
- Selling the product or service

Selling by telephone can be roughly divided into two categories: "outside" and "inside."

1. The outside salesperson sells products to his smallest

("C") accounts via the telephone, and contacts with his "A" and "B" customers and prospects.

2. The inside salesperson works on a full-time selling basis via the telephone. This is called *telemarketing*. It is used by companies whose products and markets are compatible to telephone selling. Some companies sell *entirely* through telemarketing. Others supplement the coverage of outside salespeople via telephone coverage.

Using the telephone for *all* business purposes takes considerable sales skill. Unfortunately, the telephone has become such a commonplace intrument that we are inclined to use it too casually.

In the face-to-face contact, you have a lot of things going for you. Your appearance, conduct, and personal impact are assets on which you can capitalize. The telephone contact is more difficult. You have fewer things in your favor. The words you use, and also the *way* you use those words— pronunciation, enunciation, and delivery are important. Telephone courtesies (so frequently overlooked) will help you stand out in your telephone work. Your empathy and politeness will be a welcome relief from the curtness and rudeness that is so common in telephone conversations.

The tips on telephone techniques contained in this chapter are offered to help you become more effective in your telephoning. They can be used in all types of selling, including telemarketing.

KEEP IN MIND THE VIEWPOINT
OF THE PERSON YOU ARE CALLING

Good salespeople are skilled tacticians: Tacticians study the viewpoints of the other side, and then plan their tactics accordingly.

To be successful in your telephone techniques, you must understand the problems of the person at the other end of the telephone. When you have empathy—and sympathy—for your prospect, your tactics are easier to develop and execute.

113

One of the biggest concerns of all buyers is *time*. Their time is as important to them as your time is to you. The members of top management are so concerned about time that they attend seminars to learn how to conserve time. Many keep "time logs" to list all the events of the day and the time taken for each event. They are extremely jealous of demands on their time, and this includes requests for appointments as well as the length of the calls or meetings.

This concern for time applies to managers at all levels. This is why your prospects, regardless of their rank in their organization, are extremely conscious of time. You must respect that concern or you will receive repeated "put-offs." To be effective on the telephone, it is vitally important for you to understand and accept this concern for time and to learn to cope with it. This perspective is particularly important to the salesperson when calling for an appointment.

Remember these points:

1. Your prospect probably regards telephone interruptions as serious time wasters.

2. When you ask a buyer for thirty minutes of his time, you request one sixteenth of his working day! Chances are he already has that day completely blocked out with other plans and projects.

3. He will allot you some time, carefully and reluctantly, *only* after you have earned it—after you have given him some good reasons why he should.

This is why the telephone call for an appointment requires planning. Like the sales call itself, it must be designed to make the prospect want to see you and hear your sales story. In fact, the telephone call *is* a sales talk. You plan it to do the following:

- Gain favorable attention
- Develop interest
- Create the desire to hear more
- Convince the prospect that an appointment should be made

- Get agreement as to time and place for the appointment

Your first hurdle is the secretary or staff member (if your call to the prospect is intercepted). Your first selling job is to convince the secretary that your call in important to her boss. If you fail to do this, your call can be a time waster for her—and for you.

No manager can control his time (regardless of "time logs" or any other time-saving device) unless his secretary and staff members are tuned in to his time control efforts. This is why the manager and his people are armed with "put-offs" and delaying tactics. (Remember, there is nothing personal in such tactics when applied to your call.)

Most incoming calls to your prospects are "screened." When the secretary asks, "May I ask who is calling?" or "May I ask the purpose of your call?" your call is being screened. Just as salespersons are trained in telephone techniques, secretaries are trained to screen out undesirable calls.

The *real* message in those screening questions is: "Can you give me a good reason why he should be interrupted by your phone call?"

If the secretary's next announcement is, "I am sorry, Mr. Jones is in a meeting. May I have him return your call?" you have failed to convince the "screener" that your call should be given some priority over all the many things the boss has planned for that day. And if your call is not returned today, tomorrow, or the next day, your call was 100 percent ineffective. You have not sold the screener or the prospect.

One of the screener's tactics is to divert you to another person. A common example of this is for the screener to suggest the purchasing agent as the "right man" to see concerning your product. Another diversion might be to suggest another call or a switchover to a staff person or stockroom manager. The advantages and disadvantages of such diversions will be discussed later in greater detail.

In books on effective management and in management seminars, the executive is taught to use his or her secretary (or staff member) as an "administration assistant," The secretary, in turn, is taught to conserve her boss's time in numerous ways. The four ways that concern you are:

- Monitoring (screening) incoming telephone calls
- Blocking interruptions by visitors
- Keeping appointments on schedule
- Screening incoming mail

These time conservation efforts represent the viewpoint of your prospects. This list is provided to give you a better understanding of the sales tactics required when calling for an appointment or for any other business reason.

HOW TO HANDLE PUT-OFFS AND OBJECTIONS WHEN CALLING FOR AN APPOINTMENT

When calling a prospect for an appointment, you are likely to encounter some objections and put-offs. It isn't easy to get appointments. For some calls, you have to work hard at it. You must be prepared to handle some obstacles.

In every sales office and in every company, there are certain common objections that all salespeople in the office encounter. It is smart to consult with your peers and your sales manager. Work together. Make a list of those common objections. Then have some "brainstorming" sessions. Decide among yourselves the effective answers to those objections.

After you have tested some of the suggested answers in an actual telephone sales call, "capture" them on 3″ × 5″ cue cards and shingle them (like shingles on a roof) on a piece of cardboard. Have that board handy as you call for appointments. When you get one of the expected put-offs or objections, turn to the appropriate cue card. It will remind you of the tested reply. Here are some examples:

OBJECTION: "I'm not interested.

REPLY: "Mrs. _____, I can understand your not being interested in something you have not had a chance to see, but so you can judge this idea for yourself, would you...?"

116

OBJECTION: "I'm too busy."

REPLY: "Mr. _____, I appreciate that you are a busy man; that's why I am telephoning you for an appointment rather than calling on the off-chance of seeing you. Would you...?"

PUT-OFF: "Send me literature."

REPLY: "Certainly I will send you literature, Mrs. _____, but it will be worthless unless it relates to your particular situation, and that is one of the reasons why I'd like to call on you to really understand your needs. Would you...?"

OBJECTION: "No money. Can't afford it."

REPLY: "Mr. _____, I can understand your trying to avoid unnecessary expenses; however, there is no obligation on your part. All I'm asking you to do is to look at our proposition to see whether or not it will be of value to you. Would you...?"

RULES FOR EFFECTIVE TELEPHONING

1. Think out what you are going to say.
2. Choose "power words" and "selling sentences."
3. Speak clearly, carefully, and with authority.
4. Do not permit any sign of timidity. (An indication of uncertainty will increase the chances of a put-off.)
5. Speak at a speed of from 140 to 160 words per minute.
6. Hold the mouthpiece two fingers' width away from your lips.
7. Take a deep breath before you speak.
8. Be courteous to all people along the way to your prospect—the switchboard operator, the secretary, and the staff people.
9. Check the quality of your voice by using a cassette recorder. Is your voice strong? Is it clear and pleasing?
10. Show respect for the listener's time.
11. Follow this format in planning your call:
    a. Gain favorable attention.
    b. Develop a dialogue.
    c. Make your proposal.

117

d. Handle objections.

e. Ask for the desired action.

(The actual call may not work out as planned, but at least you will be prepared.)

12. And, above all, develop and maintain an enthusiastic attitude for what you are doing. *Do your homework.* Think of the value others have enjoyed from your company's services. Reread testimonials and success stories about your company's sales. This will make you feel enthusiastic and confident in your telephone approach—and *that* attitude will be reflected in your voice and telephone manner.

RECOMMENDED COURTESIES FOR MAKING OUTGOING CALLS

Greeting	"Good morning, Mr. _____. This is John Palmer of the _____. Is it convenient for you to talk for a minute?"
	(Pause—wait for a reply—and *concentrate.* Try to sense from the tone of voice as well as the words how the prospect feels about your call. Asking "Is it convenient for you to talk for a minute?" is a rare courtesy and makes you stand out above the many callers. It makes sense to ask this question: If your propect is busy or has someone in his office, your telephone message will be wasted.)
	The prospect may reply: "No, I'm too busy to talk right now." Then say: "Okay, Mr. _____. May I call you again at, say, four o'clock?"
Be considerate	Plan what you are going to say and how you are going to say it. Be courteous but concise. Terminate the call as soon as the mission is accomplished.

Think benefits	Think and talk in terms of *what it means to the prospect—what's in it for him?*
	(Note: This is good selling and the courteous thing to do. It saves the prospect's time by getting immediately to *his* interests. It is also an effective way to "penetrate the screen.")
Close	Accomplish your mission and then close the conversation quickly and courteously by saying: "Thank you, Mr. _____. I shall get to this right away. I appreciate your time. Goodbye, Mr. _____." *Wait for him to hang up.*
Keep your promises	If you promise to keep the telephone call short, do it. If you promise to send literature, do it, and do it promptly (it is courteous to include a short, friendly note).

RECOMMENDED COURTESIES FOR COMMON SITUATIONS WHEN HANDLING *INCOMING* CALLS

Greeting	"Good morning! Acme Company, Ralph Betz speaking."
	Or if the main switchboard has taken the call,
	"Good morning! Sales Department, Ralph Betz speaking."
Placing a call on hold	"This will take me just a moment. Would you care to wait or may I call you back?"
	or
	"I have another call. Can you wait just a moment?"
	or
	"May I call you back again?"
Breaking a call on hold	"Mrs. _____ is still on the other call. Do you care to wait longer, or may I have her return your call?"

Transfer	"The _____ department would be glad to take care of this for you. May I transfer you to Mr. _____ in that department, or have him call you?"
Taking a message	"I'm sorry, he is not in. May I tell him who called?"
	or
	"I expect him at 2 o'clock. May I have him call you then? Let me be sure I have spelled your name correctly."
Shifting initiative for action	"Mr. _____ is not available right now. May I help you?"
	or
	"Mr. _____ is not available until 2 o'clock. Could Mr. _____ help you in the meantime?"
Close	"Thank you very much for calling. That will be taken care of today. Goodbye, sir."

TOOLS FOR TELEPHONING

You can save time and eliminate much confusion if you prepare yourself for your time on the telelphone. There are certain "tools" that one must have in order to do the following:

- Plan the call
- Organize for effective calls
- Execute the call
- Evaluate the call
- Follow up with the commitments made

In addition to the tools provided by your company, here are some further suggestions:

1. A *desk mirror*. Observe yourself as you talk on the phone. Smile—it relaxes the throat muscles.
2. A *cassette player* that will record your side of the conversation.
3. The *shingled cue card* set for handling objections.

120

4. The *Rolodex Petites telelphone list* of clients. The advantage of this small unit is that one can add more and more units as the call list grows. Each unit is small and doesn't take up much desk-top space.

5. *Throat spray or lozenges* (coughing and a "raspy" throat are not pleasing to the listener).

6. An *evaluation sheet* showing the customers called and the results of each call. Summarize the results at the end of each day or telephoning session. What is your ratio of appointments made to the number of calls made? As you practice your telephone techniques, is your ratio improving?

7. An *appointment book.*

8. A *telephone call record file and forms.* It is suggested that the highlights of the call be recorded at once and filed nearby for quick retrieval as needed.

9. A convenient *file folder* for easy reference—a folder for each customer and prospect—filed alphabetically.

10. *Telephone directories.*

11. Other *source material* such as manufacturer's directories, Dun and Bradstreet volumes, Moody's, association rosters, computer read-outs, and any other information to assist in the tracking down fo "suspects" and prospects.

12. *All material at hand* for the quick follow-up of customers' and prospects' requests for brochures, sales literature, personal notes, and catalogues. (When the material is readily available, it can be prepared while fresh in your mind, thus eliminating the possibility of procrastination.)

PRACTICE THESE POWER WORDS AND PHRASES FOR TELEPHONE TALKING

As previously stated, when working on the telephone, the effect on the listener is governed almost entirely by the words we use and the way we use them. We can't depend on our appearance or sales tools. The favorable impressions we achieve on the telephone must be from our:

Choice of words (vocabulary)
Pronunciation
Enunciation
Tone
Speed

It makes sense, then, to simply review the things about speech that you learned in school but to concentrate on the words and phrases you use in your work.

Much has been written on the importance of continuous vocabulary building for success in the business world. It behooves all salespersons to enlarge their vocabularies. The following words and phrases are most frequently used in dealing with your prospects and customers; use them for practice in pronunciation, enunciation, tone, and speed.

You may already be using many of the words—review them to make sure you are using them properly. Other words may not be in your vocabulary at present. Learn them, practice with them, and, in so doing, you will "program your brain" with a fresh store of words that will make your telephoning much more effective.

Here are some "idea phrases."

Mr. prospect's opinion
New product development
Mr. prospect's evaluation
Latest techniques
More effective methods
Leading business
Up to date
New development

Terms commonly used in stating a proposition

Pricing advantage	Annual consumption
Periodic calls	Attractive image
Previous month's usage	Application
Quantity discount	Account history

Responsibility	Based on customer experience,
Service	we have found...
System	Distribution center
Seasonal factor	Equipment
Turnaround time	Increase profit margins
Unique	Image
Workable inventory	Inventory control system
Anticipated needs	Literature you requested

And then we have the famous "six honest servicemen" questions that should be used in developing dialogue with your clients. Who, What, When, Where, Why, and How.

The following contains phrases that you should *not* use. They tend to irritate the prospect

Understand?	I, me, my, mine.
Get the point?	I'll tell you what!
See what I mean?	Old friend.
You don't say?	Old pal.
But honestly now	You know?
Not really ...	

The following is a list of phrases that motivate.

Will you help me?	Please.
I'm so sorry.	You were very kind.
It was my fault.	I beg your pardon.
Thank you.	It's been a great pleasure.
Gee, I'm proud of you.	I assure you.
Congratulations!	Mr. Smith ...(Use of name)

The following is a list of probing phrases.

What is your opinion?	How do you feel about ...?
What do you think?	Could you explain?
Can you illustrate?	What happened then?
What do you consider?	Why?
What were the circumstances?	Can you tell me more?

The following words invite action.

you, your	easy
money	love
save	safety
new	discovery
result	proven
health	guarantee

USE CARE IN PRONUNCIATION, ENUNCIATION, TONE, AND SPEED WHEN TALKING ON THE TELEPHONE

- *Pronunciation* is the act of uttering words, as in giving letters the correct sound and placing the accent correctly.
- *Enunciation* is to speak or pronounce *distinctly*. When you form distinct sounds, syllables, and words, you are enunciating correctly. (The *opposite* of good enunciation is *mumbling*.)
- *Tone* is the quality of a sound. It is the character, quality, and general effect of the sound of your voice.
- *Speed* is the velocity or rate of speaking.

The frame that follows contains 160 words. A good telephoning speed is speaking from 140 to 160 words per minute. Practice reading this frame. Use a cassette player or tape recorder and record your practice runs. Adjust your speed to the pace at which you are most comfortable. Judge how this speed would sound to the listener. Usually, speaking fewer than 140 words per minute is too slow for the listener—and speaking more than 160 words per minute is too fast for the listener.

Time yourself with the second hand of your watch. Clock your speeds in the practice runs.

First run	_____	Fourth run	_____
Second run	_____	Fifth run	_____
Third run	_____	Sixth run	_____

| Seventh run | ____ | Ninth run | ____ |
| Eighth run | ____ | Tenth run | ____ |

The following frame contains 160 words. (Note: You may wish to use a portion of a familiar sales brochure for this exercise.)

GREAT WAY TO SELL A HIGH-PROFIT PRODUCT!

Now you can "show and sell" packaged ice just like food. Install these beautiful merchandisers near the checkout counters for a really big turnover of one of your highest profit items.

NO SACRIFICE IN CAPACITY—Model 40 holds 115 10-pound bags of ice. Other sizes available.

FULL VIEW-cool blue interior lighting provides a fresh, clean look for added customer appreciation and response.

COMPACT—Takes up only 30 inches × 50 inches of space. Lets you set up in the mainstream of shopper traffic.

EASY INSTALLATION—Plug into standard 110V outlet. 1/4 HP compressor draws only 5.0 amps. Cold Wall design weighs only 410 lbs. (Automatic Defrost model only 450 lbs.).

AT NO CAPITAL INVESTMENT BY YOU, this unit can be installed in your store by our trained personnel. It will be regularly inspected and sericed by them—at no expense to you.

This is the way to go for quick, clean profits.

The secret of perfection in vocabulary, pronunciation, enunciation, tone, and speed is practice and more practice.

Form the habit of tape recording your side of the telephone calls. Now that you are more aware of the importance of good telephone speech, you will be pleasantly surprised as you listen to your telephone presentations. Obviously, if you detect some flaws in your vocabulary and delivery, you will want to correct yourself.

Here is one more suggestion for improving the quality of your delivery: Do not cradle the telephone receiver between your ear and your shoulder. Avoid this common method of holding the telephone receiver. It strains your vocal cords and affects your delivery.

DON'T WAIT TOO LONG
FOR A RETURN TELEPHONE CALL

You will often find yourself in a situation where you call a prospect or customer on the telephone, and someone says, "He is busy now. I'll have him return your call."

You can waste a lot of time waiting for that return call. Wait a reasonable amount of time—and only if you can find things to do for the profitable use of that time. Then don't wait any longer. Get going on another assignment. Let that return call take its natural course.

Your prospect may have other priorities that delay his return call to you, or he may be disinterested in you or your proposition. In either case, don't spend those valuable contact hours awaiting that call-back. You may fall into the trap of rationalizing away an important part of the sales day. You may reason: "I've got to stay here. I've got to keep my phone 'open'" (as you putter with nonessential details).

Go on to a strong selling stride. Take care of those call-backs at the end of a profitable sales day. You will gain a psychological advantage, and your prospect will be impressed by the fact that you didn't sweat out those waiting moments—or hours.

Tips on Making
Sales Contacts by Mail

Making contacts by mail is one of the four methods frequently neglected by salespeople. This method of contact can be placed into three classifications:

- The formal business letter
- The informal note
- Direct-mail advertisement

All three methods of contact are designed to be used by the salesperson in the field to augment the corporation's advertising and direct-mail promotions. All three methods have their place in the daily activities of the sales representative, and most mailings are designed to either precede or follow the telephone and face-to-face calls.

The tips in this chapter will augment the corporate training you have received on mail contacts. They have been field tested and proven to be effective. These suggestions can be followed by any salesperson in the field with a minimum of effort and expense.

USE THE MAGIC OF THE POSTAGE STAMP TO MAINTAIN CONTACT WITH YOUR ACCOUNTS

Use the mail as a supplement and reinforcement to your face-to-face call. Brief notes or formal business letters, mailed in between your sales calls, can serve as additional "sales calls." They can help maintain the momentum you built up during the sales interview. They can further develop your image as a true professional, one who is sincerely interested in the prospect's objectives.

Messages by mail can do the following

1. Convey additional information
2. Remind the prospect of commitments made
3. Confirm appointments or agreements
4. Ask for additional information
5. Thank or compliment the buyer
6. Make catalogs and sales brochures stand out from other promotional literature received by the prospect

Many salespersons avoid using the mail because they believe it requires a formally written business letter—and they don't have the time nor the facilities to type it. In some cases, a well-composed, dignified letter is more appropriate and *should* be used. In most cases, however, a brief, handwritten note will suffice. In fact, the a handwritten note provides the opportunity to put some personality in the message and help develop the friendly atmosphere you are trying to achieve.

It is smart to present your name to the buyer as often as possible. This must be done tactfully, without becoming obnoxious: Brief, handwritten notes can accomplish this. Their informality will not offend the buyer; they can be quickly written by the sender and easily read by the receiver; and they get the job done for both parties concerned.

A good example of the effectiveness of this informal note is when the prospect asks you to send him sales literature.

Some secretaries consider a catalog or brochure "junk mail," and place them on the bottom of the boss's mail stack. A handwritten note, however, attached to the same literature, will be placed on the top of the stack for the immediate attention of the prospect. Your personal message has made your catalog stand out and demand favorable attention. (See page 133 on the use of the "extended" calling card for the message.)

One ounce (or less) of material can be sent for the price of one first-class postage stamp (five 8 1/2 by 11-inch sheets of paper weigh one ounce). The first-class postage stamp can carry your message from the Atlantic to the Pacific—or next door to you. In either case, when properly used to reinforce your sales interview, you gain an enormous return on your investment.

BUSINESS CORRESPONDENCE IS AN IMAGE MAKER

Your business correspondence produces a tangible reflection (on paper) not only of your ability and knowledge but also of your organization's total image.

Your company spends considerable sums on advertising to promote its products and service and to create a positive image. This image may be negatively affected by carelessly prepared messages. Recipients of poorly written correspondence could have second thoughts about pursuing a business relationship with the writer and his organization. The correspondence, good or bad, is actually an exponent of your organizational style.

If there appears to be no pride in something as basic as business correspondence, it follows that there is no concern for quality of product or service—and that's a bad image. Conversely, well-written messages that convey style, expertise, and sincere interest present a good image.

But there is more than one good "corporate image" as it applies to business correspondence. One is the image that is projected by the formal business letter—the one that is typed very carefully on company stationery. This is a good image: It indicates sophistication, class, and dedication to excellence.

A second image is that of a friendly, sincere, consultative salesperson. This is also a good image: It is one created by timely, informal notes to the prospect on subjects pertinent to his needs and problems. Develop and maintain both of these images. The favorable reactions of your accounts will pay enormous dividends.

Use the formal business letter when appropriate. Also, maintain a constant flow of informal notes to prospects as well as customers. Subsequent tips in this chapter will offer help in using both kinds of business correspondence.

Building and maintaining a good image is good salesmanship, and using effective business correspondence is one way to do it.

KNOW THE ELEMENTS OF THE FORMAL BUSINESS LETTER

This tip does not attempt to completely cover the construction of a formal business letter. Chance are you have services available for producing it for you. If not, any bookstore can provide a handbook of effective business correspondence. Such a handbook should be standard issue in every business office. It will describe the following parts of a business letter:

date line	subject line
reference line	message
special mailing notations	complimentary close
on-arrival notations	identification initials
inside address	enclosure notation
attention line	carbon copy notation
salutation	postscript

Even though you have trained secretarial help available, the knowledge of these elements will help you in longhand drafting of the letter.

Draft the letter in "manuscript" style; that is, double-space between lines, triple-space between paragraphs, and provide one-inch left and right margins. This gives you room for corrections and additions. (Note: If time permits, it is smart to lay aside your first draft and reread it the next morning. You may then find better ways to convey your message.)

When you submit your draft to the office secretary, you do *not* relinquish any further responsibility. Remember, that finished letter is going to carry your signature. Make sure the letter is prepared correctly and projects your image. Make sure the stationery is of high quality. The typing must be neat and accurate, with any corrections or erasures rendered invisible. And, once again, see that the language of the letter is clear, concise, grammatically correct, and devoid of clichés. If there is any doubt about any of these points, do it over. That letter must support the good impression you made when you were face to face with your prospect. Carelessness in drafting or sloppy typing can ruin the good work you have done so far.

HOW TO DESIGN
THE BUSINESS LETTER THAT SELLS

Letters that sell the product, arrange a meeting (for the purpose of selling the product), get an appointment, or get some other desired action are called "selling letters." They must be planned and composed as carefully as you would plan a sales call.

Before you start drafting your letter, do some charting of Benefits and Features and Poor Features and Losses (refer to the forms described in Chapter 6). Write the features of your proposition, and then the benefits your prospect will enjoy from them. Do the same with the prospect's present course of action. Write its poor features and the losses he is incurring. This exercise will crystallize your thinking. You are now ready to start drafting your letter.

Think of the letter in terms of five "building blocks" as follows:

Gaining favorable attention. After the usual salutation, write a paragraph designed to gain the reader's attention. A powerful selling sentence, for example, is a good attention getter. It should be derived from your charting exercise. For example: "I have an idea that will help you increase your production and save you money."

Holding interest. In this "building block," hold your prospect's interest by expanding on the opening sentence. Add additional benefits.

Making the proposal. In this paragraph, give a clear, concise explanation of your proposition. Specifically, what do you want the prospect to do and why should he do it?

Handling objections. You can't, of course, hear the objections, but you *can* anticipate some. In this paragraph, make strong points that will allay the prospect's possible fears.

Asking for the desired action. Before you started your draft, you had a clear objective to be achieved by the letter—an appointment, a purchase, or some other desired action. In this paragraph, ask for it.

Finish the letter with a complimentary close.

Some letters require follow-ups, usually in the form of a telephone call. Put the copy in your tickler (reminder) file for the suitable follow-up date. Reread your copy before calling the prospect for the decision you have requested.

Once again, one of the keys to *all* sales contacts is good planning—and this is particularly true for the business letter that is designed to sell.

AVOID UNNECESSARY WORDS
AND OVERWORKED CLICHÉS

The busy prospect (or customer) will appreciate clarity and brevity in your communications to him. Therefore, avoid unnecessary words and overworked clichés. He will get your message faster—and you will get better results.

Here are some examples of stale, awkward expressions that should be avoided—as well as suggestions for alternatives:

132

Avoid	*Alternative*
As per your request	As you requested
We acknowledge receipt of	We have your
Due to the fact that	Because
We beg to acknowledge	Thank you for
Your letter dated July 1	Your July 1st letter
Hoping for the favor of a reply	May I hear from you soon
We are of the opinion	We think
Reduce to a minimum	Minimize
Subsequent to our interview	After our interview

These examples are offered to "whet your appetite." Be on the alert for better improvements in your writing style. Most handbooks of effective business correspondence will provide many additional examples of superfluous or hackneyed expressions.

Make your messages easy to read—and you will get positive messages in return.

USE AN 'EXTENDED' CALLING CARD FOR PERSONAL NOTES TO ACCOUNTS

Busy prospects and customers first look at personal mail—and then brochures and advertising "when they get time."

One way to get attention to your mailings is to attach a personal, handwritter note. It attracts special, favorable attention. In fact, it *demands* attention.

The message form you use can be an "extension" of your calling card (see figure 9–1).

This provides the same information about you that's contained in your business card plus additional space for a handritten message. It tells it all: who you are, who you represent, your title, your product, and your message.

The production of these extended calling cards doesn't have to be elaborate. You can produce them on a local basis, at minimal expense, through the use of local fast-printing services. Taping three of your business cards on a sheet of 8 1/2 by 11-inch paper will give you the "master" from which hundreds of copies can be made. (See Figure 9–2.)

FIGURE 9–1   Extended calling card

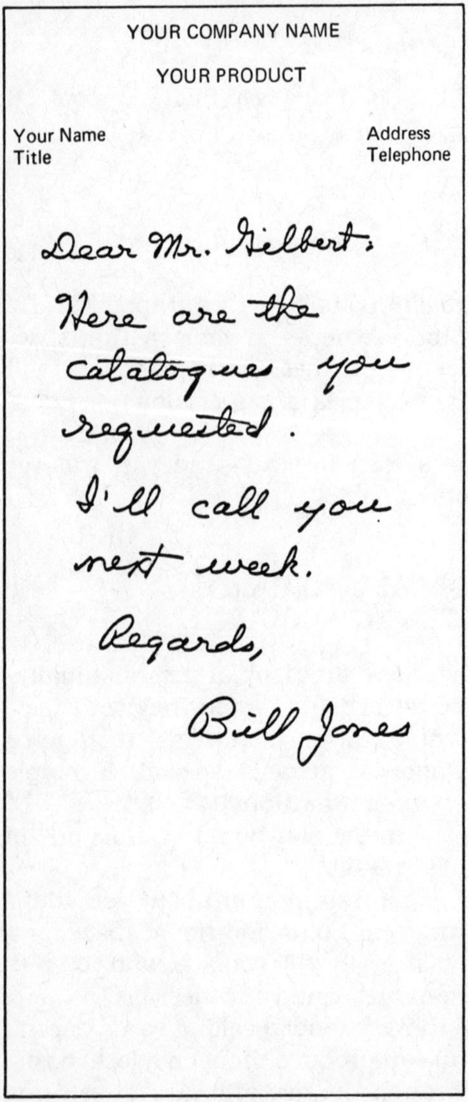

YOUR COMPANY NAME

YOUR PRODUCT

Your Name   Address
Title   Telephone

Dear Mr. Gilbert,
Here are the
catalogues you
requested.
I'll call you
next week.
Regards,
Bill Jones

FIGURE 9–2 Extended calling card master

YOUR COMPANY NAME

YOUR PRODUCT

Your Name
Title

Address
Telephone

YOUR COMPANY NAME

YOUR PRODUCT

Your Name
Title

Address
Telephone

- cut here

YOUR COMPANY NAME

YOUR PRODUCT

Your Name
Title

Address
Telephone

- cut here

USE INDIVIDUAL CATALOGUE PAGES
TO YOUR ADVANTAGE

Many catalogues contain descriptions of items that are not pertinent to a specific case. When you send a propect a complete catalogue, the information about the items of his special interest can be lost in the maze of material. Further, heavy catalogues cause high postage expense.

Some items in your product line can be placed into special interest groups. For example, some products may be ideal for hospitals, others for banks, and still others for manufacturers. Individual pages of product information for each interest group will get closer attention from the prospect than the hundreds of pages in the complete catalogue.

Also, many catalogue pages can be easily duplicated by a local printing-while-you-wait offset print shop. Fifty or one hundred copies can be produced at a minimal cost. Two catalogue pages can be printed on the front and back of a single sheet of paper, thus saving postage expense. Five pages containing ten pages of product descriptions can be mailed for the price of one first-class stamp.

The preparation for the printing operation is easy and can be completed in less than one hour. Here is how:

1. Start with your company letterhead—which is usually 8½ by 11 inches. Cut the selected catalogue page to fit on the letterhead sheet, leaving the letterhead exposed. (Note: in lieu of a letterhead, you can tape your calling card at the top of a blank sheet of paper.)

2. Use transparent tape to fasten the catalogue page to the letterhead sheet. That page is now ready for printing. It contains all the pertinent information: what the product is, what it does, how much it costs, and where to buy it (indicated by the letterhead).

3. When you print both sides of the letterhead, leave some room on each side at the lower right corner for the notation: "See the reverse side for information on an additional item." Also, attach a personal note or business card so the resulting order is credited to *you*.

This is one more suggestion to help you get more sales production through the use of contacts by mail.

10

Tips on the Formal, Written Proposal

The fourth type of contact with prospects and customers is in the form of the written proposal.

The purchase of many products requires multiple decisions. This may be because the use of the product involves two or more departments; another possible reason is the high price of the product or service. Many companies require "committee buying" when the dollar amount exceeds a certain figure.

When these or similar conditions occur, the person you are dealing with will tell you to give him some written (or printed) details. That means that he needs some information to present to either several executives or the "buying committee." If that individual doesn't do this very often, he may be unsure of what he really wants from you. He may not call it a proposal. He is likely to call it "something in writing."

Further, he may not know how to effectively handle the information after he receives it from you.

All of this means that if he doesn't know what he wants—and if you don't know what to give him—your sales could go down the drain.

This chapter is devoted to "proposal selling"—a very important subject for most salespeople.

A WRITTEN PROPOSAL
IS A SALES PRESENTATION
—PLAN IT CAREFULLY

"Proposal selling" is one of the most neglected sales techniques. This is unfortunate, and results in a serious waste of sales effort. A well-planned, written proposal—when required—is vital to the success of a sale, yet many salespeople neglect its use.

The need for a written proposal is indicated when the prospect says: "Put something in writing and I'll take it up with my management." At this point, the salesperson reaches a "fork in the road to the sale" (See Figure 10–1).

FIGURE 10–1   A "fork in the road" to the sale

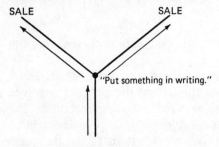

He can take the left road, which is the better choice, by replying to the prospect: "We have a detailed story to tell your management. Let me help you present it." This is the safer way; if permitted, the sales representative maintains control of his proposition, He or she makes the presentation to management just the way he feels it should be made.

But frequently the prospect answers: "No, we have a closed meeting every Monday morning. Put something in the mail and I'll explain your proposition to the group." Now the salesperson must take the other road. It's not as desirable as the "left road," but it can still lead to the sale—if handled properly.

The second road to the sale is taken by writing a formal proposal. At this point, many salespeople make a common mistake and lose the sale: They simply follow the prospect's suggestion by "just dropping something in the mail." They mail a descriptive sales brochure with a note—and wait for a positive reply. It seldom works.

A formal, written proposal is more than a description of the product. In fact, the proposal is a sales presentation in writing—for someone else to present. And that "someone else" is seldom trained in selling. Therefore, the success of the sale is dependent on the completeness of the written proposal.

The following is a proven format for a powerful written proposal.

1. Usual greetings and expressions of appreciation for the opportunity to submit a proposal.
2. A review of the prospect's present course of action (the product in use and present methods)—and a tactful reminder of losses being incurred.
3. A complete description of the better course (the new product or method). This must be heavily loaded with benefits, features, and "selling sentences." It serves two purposes:
   a. To sell the new proposition
   b. To force the prospect to review the poor features and losses of his present course of action.
4. The details of price, delivery, and shipping information.
5. A clear explanation of the return on investment.
6. A positive and forceful request for the order.
7. Courtesies of the close.

The proposal should be carefully prepared and typed. Many organizations provide their salespeople with a handsome brochure or binder to house the proposal.

It is smart to hand deliver the proposal. This gives the sales representative a chance to:

1. Ask again for permission to make the presentation to the buying group.
2. If this suggestion is not accepted, tactfully coach the prospect on the most effective methods for presenting the proposal to his colleagues.

Follow this advice the next time your prospect says, "Put something in writing." It will definitely improve your chances for the sale.

DEVELOP A LIBRARY
OF STANDARD PARAGRAPHS
THAT CAN BE USED IN ALL PROPOSALS

There is no point in starting from "scratch" for each proposal. There are certain paragraphs in many proposals that are similar, and those paragraphs can be standardized. They can be adapted, with perhaps some modifications, for subsequent proposals.

Some sales offices maintain a file of successful proposals. These can be studied and used as patterns for the new proposal. Many sales offices maintain a library of sample *paragraphs*; in fact, some code number the paragraphs for easy instruction to the typist. For example, the library may contain a large selection of opening paragraphs. In the draft for the new proposal, the salesperson simply writes instructions to the typist, such as "use 0–6." The typist would then copy from the sample paragraph "0–6." The same procedure applies to other paragraphs throughout the many proposals presented by the company to its prospects.

Once again, it is a waste of time to "reinvent the wheel" for each proposal. Think of a proposal as being constructed from a series of "building blocks" or paragraphs. Some of those paragraphs can be used again and again for additional proposals.

With a library of successsful paragraphs and complete proposals, your job is made easier. You are therefore moti-

140

vated to do more proposal selling. In many instances, selling by proposal in vital to your success. Make sure you don't miss a good sale because of a poorly written or incomplete proposal.

PROVIDE COPIES OF YOUR PROPOSAL FOR ALL MEMBERS OF THE "BUYING COMMITTEE"

This is important. Don't leave anything to chance. The individual with whom you are working may be inexperienced in this type of sales situation. He may simply read your proposal to his committee. Some participants may make notes and "catch" a few key points; others will notice other salient points. Rarely do *all* those in attendance hear and retain the complete proposal.

To guard against this problem, supply your prospect (the individual) with a copy for every person who attends the meeting. Suggest that he distribute the copies immediately *after* he has read your proposal. During the discussion that follows the reading, each participant can scan your proposal, and get "caught up" on its details. (If your prospect is *really* alert, he will go back over your proposal after the reading so that he is certain that all those present really understand all the details.)

Proposal writing is difficult. The effective presentation of the written proposal is even *more* difficult because it is usually done by an inexperienced person. Recognize this problem and do everything you can to make the presentation effective.

FOLLOW UP ON YOUR PROPOSAL

Never let your proposal dangle. Follow up on it *immediately* after the meeting. Even if your proposal was well received, your prospect may not feel the need to get back to you immediately after the decision. *Don't let that decision go stale*. It is psychologically important to put it into action at once. There are two reasons for this:

- If you don't vigorously follow up your proposal, your prospect may get the idea that it's not very important to you.

- If your prospect isn't spurred into quick action, some natural procrastination can set in. Other things can demand his attention, and *your* project is soon put on the "back burner."

A professional, complete proposal deserves prompt attention from both the buyer and the seller. You are being unfair to yourself when you don't follow up quickly and confidently.

Tips on Methods
for Performance
Evaluation

Performance evaluation is psychologically important to you. It may be important to others, but it is even more important to *you*—and your attitude.

As stated earlier in this book, *attitude* is one of the six major segments of a sales training program. This attitude must come from within. No one can teach you the right attitude for what you are doing; yet, a good attitude is vital to your success. Therefore, you must build your own attitude.

Selling is a lonely business. You must recognize this. You must accept the fact that much of your development and success must come from within you.

Good salespeople are competitive. That's what makes them good sales producers. In a competitive situation, you always measure your progress against that of another person—or against your own record. Of course, you can always watch the sales production of your peers and compare it to yours. There is nothing wrong with that. In fact, it's healthy.

But the *real* measure of progress is that of your current performance against your previous sales production statistics. This is an evaluation of performance in the same territory, under the same logistical conditions, with the same products, the same markets, and *by the same salesperson.* In effect, it is a real raw measurement of your personal development as a professional salesperson. Such a measurement is a challenge to you.

The following tips are offered as suggestions for self-measurement. The instruments you use for doing this can be for "your eyes only"—but realize that they are the most important "eyes" in your self-development.

ANALYZE YOUR SALES CALL

One of the marks of a professional is his or her willingness to evaluate results. This is true of athletes, doctors, engineers, and all others who strive for excellence in their work.

The true sales professional reviews the sales call *immediately* upon completion. It takes courage and self-discipline to do this. An objective critique may reveal some faults that have previously gone unnoticed. This is particularly true when calling repeatedly on the same customer. It is easy to become careless when dealing with friendly accounts.

The Sales Call Planner on page 93 can also be used as a tool for your self-analysis. Use it in "playing back" your sales call. Ask yourself these questions:

- Did I have clear objectives for that call?
- Did I *really* gain favorable attention?
- Did I develop a worthwhile dialogue? Did I determine the prospect's needs?
- Was my proposal presented in terms of benefits? Did I use powerful selling sentences?
- How did I handle the objections? Was I *really* prepared for them?
- What action did I expect? Did I get it? How could I have done better in getting the desired action?

144

- Were my sales tools adequate? Did I handle them smoothly and professionally?

This type of objective review will set the stage for improvement—call by call—and your "batting average" will measure the results.

ANALYZE YOUR CALL REPORTS
—AND CORRECT ANY WEAKNESSES
THEY MAY DISCLOSE

Form the habit of analyzing your call reports every month or quarter. It is smart time and territory management. Your review of a number of call reports will give you an accurate picture of your activities—and the results of your efforts. When you don't analyze your sales work, you can easily overlook a trend that could be leading to some problems.

The summary (the analysis report to yourself) should be on a single sheet for quick, easy reading. The new summary sheet should be laid beside those from several previous periods. This combination gives you an even broader perspective from which you can spot good things and bad things in your operations.

The sample summary sheet shown in Figure 11–1 shows some of the key factors to look for in analyzing your sales activities. Your company's official call report form may not include some of this information. Add a supplemental form of your own for the additional items. If you wish, this summary or analysis can be "for your eyes only."

Doing this type of business analysis is good training for a promotion. It is what sales managers must do for effective strategic planning and sales leadership.

Some statistics may "leap off" the analysis sheet at you and trigger immediate corrective action. The number of calls per day, number of calls on new accounts, number of booked sales to new accounts, and average cost per order can reveal disturbing weaknesses. To the conscientious territory manager, these numbers are signals indicating trends that must be dealt with.

Once again, the call report (that is usually written so grudgingly) can be of more importance to *you* than to management. It is the source from which a very powerful analysis

FIGURE 11–1 Form for "Analysis of the Information in My Call Reports"

SALES REPRESENTATIVE:

For period from _____ to _____ , 19___	
(____ months)	

1. Number of days worked in this period ☐

2. Number of calls made in this period ☐

   a. Number of calls made on new accounts (new business) ☐

   b. Number of calls made on established customers ☐

3. Average number of calls per day ☐

4. Total booked sales $☐

   a. Total booked sales to new accounts (new business) $☐

   b. Total booked sales to established customers $☐

5. Total direct cost of sales (salary, commission and travel) $☐

6. Total orders booked ☐

7. Average direct cost per order $☐

My comments concerning this analysis and the corrective action (if any) required:

_____

_____

_____

_____

_____

_____

_____

_____

_____

can be made. The analysis, in turn, can be the guide for strategic planning and possible redirecting of sales efforts.

The professional analyzes his or her performance—frequently and objectively.

KEEP A "TIME LOG" FOR A WEEK OR TWO TO SEE HOW YOU USED YOUR CONTACT HOURS

Please refer to Figure 11–2, which shows the form titled How I Used My Contact Hours. The form displays fifteen-minute segments from 8 A.M. to 6 P.M. for every day of the work week. This form is an effective measuring tool: Ten photocopies will give you a two-week supply of daily reports to yourself.

The summary at the end of each day could show strengths and weaknesses in your management of contact hours. A common weakness, for example, is spending too much time with "C" accounts. Another common fault is to plan the driving inefficiently, thus spending too much time in travel.

COMPARE YOUR SALES COSTS TO YOUR SALES RESULTS

It is smart to think about your cost of sales in relation to your sales production. Be sure to do this, even though sales costs have little direct influence on your present income.

As you measure your sales costs, you develop an important management perspective. You learn to *think* like a manager; in essence, you *are* a manager—of your territory. Knowing your sales costs helps you set priorities. It guides you to the accounts and the parts of your territory that will yield a greater return on your investment of selling time.

What are sales costs? To top management, sales costs include many things, such as advertising, cost of goods sold, sales management expense, and overhead. To *you*, as a territory manager, direct sales costs are:

1. Sales man-hour expense
2. Car expense
3. Other travel expense

Sales man-hour expense and car expense can be easily calculated and used as standard units of measure. "Other travel expense" can be added up each day and used to figure the cost of that day's work.

Sales man-hour expense is the total of your salary, commissions, bonuses, and fringe benefits added up for the

FIGURE 11–2   Form for "How I Used My Contact Hours"

Salesperson_____ Day_____ Date_____

| Time | Sales Calls | | | | | | | | | | OTHER DUTIES |
| | Customers | | | Prospects | | | | | | | |
	A	B	C	A	B	C	TR	WA	EN	TE	
8:00 to 8:15 a.m.											
8:15 to 8:30											
8:30 to 8:45											
8:45 to 9:00											
9:00 to 9:15											
9:15 to 9:30											
9:30 to 9:45											
9:45 to 10:00											
10:00 to 10:15											
10:15 to 10:30											
10:30 to 10:45											
10:45 to 11:00											
11:00 to 11:15											
11:15 to 11:30											
11:30 to 11:45											
11:45 to 12:00 noon											
12:00 to 12:15 p.m.											
12:15 to 12:30											
12:30 to 12:45											
12:45 to 1:00											
1:00 to 1:15											
1:15 to 1:30											
1:30 to 1:45											
1:45 to 2:00											
2:00 to 2:15											
2:15 to 2:30											
2:30 to 2:45											
2:45 to 3:00											
3:00 to 3:15											
3:15 to 3:30											
3:30 to 3:45											
3:45 to 4:00											
4:00 to 4:15											
4:15 to 4:30											
4:30 to 4:45											
4:45 to 5:00											
5:00 to 5:15											
5:15 to 5:30											
5:30 to 5:45											
5:45 to 6:00											
TOTAL TIME											
% OF DAY											

CODE: TR – Travel Time   TE – Telephone Contacts
        WA – Waiting Time   Other Duties – those not listed
        EN – Entertainment and Lunch   in the columns

Your analysis of your use of the contact hours _____
_____

Corrective action required (if any) _____
_____

full year and divided by the total annual contact hours (2082 in most cases). In Figure 11–3, the sales man-hour cost of $15.00 is used.

    Car expense is the annual car leasing, insurance, maintenance, and operating costs for the full year divided by the total annual mileage. Your sales manager can give you an accurate estimate. In Figure 11–4, the figure of 20 cents per mile is used.

FIGURE 11–3 Sales call planner and report

SALES REPRESENTATIVE _____ DATE _____

TERRITORY SECTOR WORKED _____

CALLS PLANNED	CALLS MADE	TAKE TO CALL	RESULTS OF CALL	SALES MADE $
TOTALS				

TIME AND COST ESTIMATES

Number of calls made today _____

Average time per call
(total hours [   ]
divided by number of calls _____

Average cost of my time
per call (my hourly cost
[   ] x [   ] average hours
per call) _____

Average travel expense
per call (see the column
on the right) _____

Average cost per call _____

Average sale per call $ _____

Car mileage reading
(finish of the day) _____

Car mileage reading
(start of the day) _____

Total car mileage
for the day @ _____

Total car expense _____

Other travel expense
for the day _____

Total travel expense
for the day _____

Average travel
expense per call _____

149

FIGURE 11-4 Completed sales call planner and report

SALES REPRESENTATIVE _Jim Gilbert_ DATE _1/16/_
TERRITORY SECTOR WORKED _Central Sector_

CALLS PLANNED	CALLS MADE	TAKE TO CALL	RESULTS OF CALL	SALES MADE $
Acme Co.	✓	Proposal + sales literature	Looks good. Go back 2/2	
Jones + McLaughlin		Sales brochures	Couldn't see me.	
Piper + Son	✓	Discount schedule + quotation	Got the order	2,293⁰⁰
United Transformer	✓	Lunch with Bill Madison	Sold 6 units - more later	8,494⁰⁰
Standard Appliance	✓	Fresh catalogues + visuals	Be back next week! See his boss.	
Brown + Adams Co.	✓	3 sets of proposals	Considering the proposal - looks very good	
W. W. Grinder, Inc.	✓	Brochure + sample of new attachment	Sold a dozen more later	6,493⁸⁵
Wentworth Corp.	✓	Visuals + literature.	Make survey of their assembly line needs (March)	
TOTALS	**7**			17,580⁸⁵

TIME AND COST ESTIMATES

Number of calls made today _7_

Average time per call (total hours [8½] divided by number of calls _1.21_

Average cost of my time per call (my hourly cost [15⁰⁰] x [1.21] average hours per call) _#16⁸⁰_

Average travel expense per call (see the column on the right) _3²³_

Average cost per call _20⁰³_

Average sale per call _$2,511⁵⁵_

Car mileage reading (finish of the day) _8,765_

Car mileage reading (start of the day) _8,711_

Total car mileage for the day @ 20¢ _54_

Total car expense _10⁸⁰_

Other travel expense for the day Tel. .60 / Lunch 11.20 / 11.80

Total travel expense for the day _22⁶⁰_

Average travel expense per call _3²³_

Other travel expense consists of all allowable costs such as hotels, meals, tolls, telephone, and entertainment of prospects. Figure 11-5 shows how these expenses are added up for each sales day.

Figures 11-3, 11-4, and 11-5 illustrate how factors such as distance traveled and number of calls made can make a substantial difference in your cost per call. The arithmetic used in the examples may not apply to your operation,

FIGURE 11-5 Completed sales call planner and report

SALES REPRESENTATIVE _Jim Gillert_   DATE _1/17/_

TERRITORY SECTOR WORKED _Northeast Sector_

CALLS PLANNED	CALLS MADE	TAKE TO CALL	RESULTS OF CALL	SALES MADE $
Johnson & Johnson	✓	Proposals & specifications	Sold 3 units	4,650.00
Meade & Co.		Sales literature	Couldn't see me.	
Case Mfg.	✓	Visuals & demonstrator	Looks good - go back in March	
Bellow Mfg.		Proposal & survey results		
Phillips, Inc.	✓	Lunch with Craig Phillips	Sold 2 units	2,960.00
TOTALS	3			7,610.00

TIME AND COST ESTIMATES

Number of calls made today   _3_

Average time per call (total hours [8½] divided by number of calls _2.83_

Average cost of my time per call (my hourly cost [15.00] x [2.83] average hours per call) _$42.50_

Average travel expense per call (see the column on the right) _15.27_

Average cost per call _57.77_

Average sale per call _$2,536.67_

Car mileage reading (finish of the day) _8930_

Car mileage reading (start of the day) _8765_

Total car mileage for the day @ 20¢ _165_

Total car expense _33.00_

Other travel expense for the day   Tolls 2.20   Lunch 10.60   12.80

Total travel expense for the day _45.80_

Average travel expense per call _15.27_

but the principle remains the same. (Incidentally, the form used in Figures 11-1 and 11-2, for time and cost estimates can also be used as a call planner and call report.)

When you are constantly aware of your sales costs in ratio to your sales production, you will be alert to the need for the following:

1. Making every call more effective.

2. Making more effective calls in the sales day.
3. Concentrating on the richest sectors of your territory that will produce more sales at less cost.
4. Routing yourself more efficiently to reduce driving time during contact hours.
5. Performing nonselling tasks during nonselling hours.

A SIMPLE SALES PRODUCTION CHART
CAN BE A SELF-MOTIVATOR

It's always a good idea to be able to answer your own question: "How am I doing?" A simple chart can give you that answer at a glance. Most professional salespeople maintain records of their sales production in relation to their sales goals. If their companies don't provide record forms, they make their own.

A sales progress chart can be easy to contrive. Chart paper can be purchased at a nominal cost from any stationery store. A single sheet of paper can report your monthly sales for twenty-four months (two years). The form shown in Figure 11–6 may serve your needs.

Here is how to make the chart work for you. On the left, plot the possible monthly sales. For example, if your *average* monthly sales are $5,000, print "$5,000" on the *sixth* horizontal line. On the lines below that, print $4,000, $3,000, $2,000, $1,000 and $0, respectively. On the lines *above* the $5,000, print $6,000, $7,000, $8,000 and $9,000, respectively. That gives you room on the chart to report $4,000 above your average. Now, plot your monthly sales quota using a heavy horizontal line. That is your minimum sales goal.

It is usually better to chart "booked" business rather than "billed" business. Booked business consists of new, *valid* orders. These must be *firm* orders, not vague promises. When you keep your eye on your daily *booked* business, the *billed* business will take care of itself. (There is sometimes a two- or three-month processing time to convert a booked order to a billed sale.)

FIGURE 11–6 Sales production–progress chart

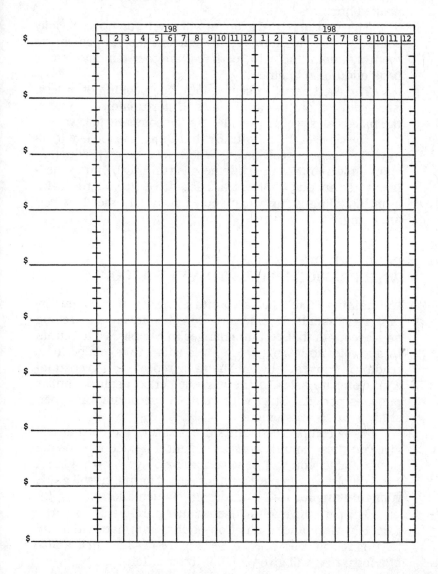

Keep a daily record in your diary of booked business, and then, at least once a week, plot the figures on the vertical line for the current month. As you watch that solid line crawl upward, you will have a running record of your progress in booked business.

This type of record keeping will psych you up, especially when the vertical chart for the current month passes the monthly quota line with, perhaps, another ten days left to book additional business.

The excitement in selling is in the booking of orders. Keep your eye on that at all times. Unfortunately, for many, the billed sales record provided by the company follows well after the close of the month. By that time, it is too late to do anything about weak sales. When your sales production chart shows your booked business is running behind schedule, you can add that extra sales drive *during* the sales month. Selling is fun when you know at all times how you are doing.

COMPARE CURRENT SALES
WITH PREVIOUS SALES TO A KEY ACCOUNT

Maintaining established accounts is one of your most important assignments. It is possible to get so involved in selling *new* accounts that certain changes in established accounts escape your notice. Therefore, it is smart to take a periodic reading of your established business (repeat sales to customers). Compare sales in the current period against similar previous periods. Start with your "A" accounts, and then study your "B" customers.

Many companies maintain customer records that will give you these comparisons at a glance. If such records are not available, you will be wise to develop your own. Figure 11–7 displays a sample customer record form that will guide your thinking for your own design of such a form.

The periodic reading of customer purchases is another form of performance evaluation—*your* performance in maintaining repeat sales volume. See Figure 11–8 for an example of a form that will give you that information.

FIGURE 11-7 Customer record

CUSTOMER RECORD

TELEPHONE ( ) _____

COMPANY _____

ADDRESS _____

CITY _____ STATE _____ ZIP _____

EXECUTIVES _____ TITLE _____

_____ _____

_____ _____

_____ _____

KEY PRODUCTS PURCHASED AND THEIR APPLICATIONS

_____

_____

_____

_____

_____

NOTES ON PROBLEMS, TRENDS, LIKES, DISLIKES

_____

_____

_____

_____

_____

_____

_____

SALES COMPARISONS

1st 6 Months 19__	2nd 6 Months 19__	1st 6 Months 19__	2nd 6 Months 19__
PRODUCT A - $	PRODUCT A - $	PRODUCT A - $	PRODUCT A - $
PRODUCT B - $	PRODUCT B - $	PRODUCT B - $	PRODUCT B - $
PRODUCT C - $	PRODUCT C - $	PRODUCT C - $	PRODUCT C - $
PRODUCT D - $	PRODUCT D - $	PRODUCT D - $	PRODUCT D - $
TOTAL $_____	TOTAL $_____	TOTAL $_____	TOTAL $_____

SEE REVERSE SIDE

155

FIGURE 11–8 Customer purchase record

1st Half 19__		2nd Half 19__		1st Half 19__		2nd Half 19__	
Date	Amount	Date	Amount	Date	Amount	Date	Amount

COMPARE YOUR PERFORMANCE
WITH THE ASSIGNMENTS
LISTED IN YOUR JOB DESCRIPTION

Another method of performance evaluation is to compare what you have done to what you have been paid to do.

The company's description of your job lists the terms and conditions of your assignment as a salesperson. Most job descriptions clearly state what you are expected to do, and your compensation is usually based on the company's expectations for the completion of those assignments.

Many sales managers use the job description as a basis for evaluating the salesperson's actual performance. This performance evaluation is usually conducted at least once a year. It creates a good climate for a frank discussion between the sales representative and the sales manager.

Don't wait for that annual performance evaluation to evaluate your performance: Do it for yourself much more frequently. Reread your job description paragraph by paragraph. For each assignment, ask yourself the following questions:

Am I carrying out this assignment as my company expects me to do?

How can I do my work better?

Evaluate your own performance three or four times a year. You will then be well prepared for your sales manager's evaluation of you and your work.

Tips on Paperwork and Office Routine

Sales work creates paperwork, such as communications, order handling, service, and routine follow-ups.

Even though you have support services available to you, there are still certain tasks that only you can handle. They are all part of the personal service you offer your accounts and your company. The tips in this chapter will give you some ideas that will help you perform those tasks. Following these tips may smooth out your office routine and allow you even more selling time.

MAINTAIN OPEN COMMUNICATIONS

Open communications from and to the field are vital in any sales organization. Your reports on your sales activities provide important information to corporate headquarters. When combined with the reports from your fellow salespeople, your marketing executives at "the home office" get a clear picture of field conditions. With this information, they can then plan strategy and tactics that will eventually help you as well as your company.

When you don't understand the reason for paperwork, you might procrastinate in doing it. However, realize that it *is* important and you *should* do it—completely and on time. As a territory manager, you play an important part in your company's communication system.

As a *time* manager, open communications can be of great assistance to you. You use your backup team when special expertise is needed. Good reports and open communications alert the backup teams; your information gives them the facts they need to properly assist you. Special assistance, when required, will conserve your time and make you more effective.

Your daily call report is an excellent example of a good communication tool. It tells the various levels of management what is going on in your territory. Of equal importance is the call report, which tells you what you are doing right and what you are doing wrong. (A monthly or quarterly analysis of your reports will "communicate" to you a broad picture of your own activities.)

Your customer is another important link in the communication system. He is a "sender" and a "receiver." He can give you facts about industry trends, competition, and quality problems that should be quickly communicated to your management. Also, it is important to him that you keep him informed about pricing, shipping problems, and trends that will help him do a better job of buying.

You are the hub of a communication system that transmits and receives information—to management, to your customers, to your backup teams, and to your peers. Keep those lines of communication open by doing your part.

FOLLOW UP ALL COMMITMENTS MADE TO CUSTOMERS AND PROSPECTS

A professional's word is his bond. You are a professional, and your promise is a commitment. You are honor-bound to keep it—as promised—and on time.

One of the first things to remember about commitments is that they must be realistic: They must be according to company policy, and they must be practical and possible.

It is easy to "overpromise." As you near the close of the sale, it is tempting to make commitments that can't be met. You may make promises hurriedly, and without thinking first, so that the order is not jeopardized.

Such overpromising can start a chain reaction of claims, counterclaims, bickering, quarreling, frustrations, permanent distrust, and customer animosity. It isn't worth it. In fact, it's downright unethical—as well as expensive. Making commitments that can't be met is poor salesmanship. *Don't do it!*

A legitimate and realistic commitment is another matter. You are on safe ground when you make a promise within the framework of company policy. When you do that, you can expect the full support of your management and backup teams.

There are, however, many possibilities of human error. It is up to you to see that the commitment is met. Here is where a tickler file, good communications, and a sincere desire to service the account are vital to the scheduled meeting of that commitment. The key to "commitment meeting" is attitude: You must *care* about your account; you must *care* about your reputation; and you must *care* about upholding the honor and reputation of your company.

Successful following up on your promises can be very rewarding, and very profitable. Customers are hungry for that extra-special service. When they get it, they spread the word to other prospective customers.

Make commitments that can be met, and see that they *are* met. Your rewards will be solid repeat business, enthusiastic customers, and, last but not least, an inner satisfaction that is psychologically rewarding.

FOLLOW THESE SUGGESTIONS
FOR HANDLING OFFICE WORK

Here are some ideas that will help you with those routine office chores. If you work out of a company office, some of this work may be done for you. Even if you *do* have an office, it is a good idea to set up additional working facilities at home.

Office work (paperwork) is part of your job, and it must be done carefully and on time. You have probably seen or experienced incidences in which the mishandling of paperwork has caused inconvenience to the customer and possibly lost business. Conversely, you have seen efficient handling of paperwork that resulted in excellent order handling and praise from the customers.

The following suggestions apply to setting up facilities in your home. Some of them may also apply to your company office. First of all, you need a spot you can call your own, whether it's in the attic, the basement, or a spare bedroom. You don't need a lot of fancy office furniture, but there are some basic items you should have: A list of these follows:

1. A good, well-lighted *work surface*. The standard 30 by 60 inch desk is about right. A card table will do.
2. A small *filing cabinet*. A metal file is preferred (a two-drawer type), but a Banker's Box cardboard file will do.
3. A *portable file* that you can carry back and forth to your car.
4. A supply of *manila file folders*.
5. A *Roladex file* for addresses and telephone numbers. (A Roladex Petite version can be kept in a desk drawer. You can add more petites as needed.)
6. A *tickler file* with twelve monthly folders and thirty-one daily folders. (Note: A "tickler file" consists of forty-three file folders. Thirty-one files are numbered for days, and twelve are labeled for months. You insert reminder notes in the *months* in which you plan action. For the current month, you reassign the reminder notes to the *days* on which you plan action.)
7. A large twelve-month *wall planning calendar*.
8. A supply of *memo pads, report forms*, and *envelopes*.
9. Desk-top items such as *pens, paper clips, stapler, cellophane tape*, and a supply of *memo forms*.
10. A small *alphabetical file* large enough to accommodate your memos.

Make up a file folder for each of your accounts. Place in each folder all pertinent data such as order cards, memos, correspondence, and customer information. Place these folders in your filing cabinet alphabetically or according to route. The key to good filing is *retrieval*—will you be able to find the material quickly when you want it?

The reason for poor filing and slow retrieval is *procrastination*. There is a tendency to put the material down, to be filed later. But that is bad time management. File every piece of paper as soon as you get it.

When You Get Home

Look at your phone messages and open your mail. Handle each piece of paper only once; either file it, act on it, or throw it away. If you can't do something about it immediately, write across it what you *plan* to do about it. Then place it in your tickler file under the month and day when you *will* do something about it. Complete all memos and reports before you relax for the evening. All this takes self-discipline—but it will pay dividends.

The small alphabetical file previously mentioned is for memos. Carry a supply of memo forms with you. They can serve as adjuncts to your customer records. Make notes to yourself of things to do for certain customers, and file them as soon as you return to your home. Also, have that file near your telephone so you can make notes of telephone conversations. When you receive calls from customers, you can quickly retrieve notes of previous calls and "tune in" quickly to the new call.

Preparing for Tomorrow's Work

To save time tomorrow, prepare the evening before by doing the following:

1. Pull the files on tomorrow's calls; look through them to refresh your memory, and jot down key information you will need.

2. Look at your tickler file under tomorrow's date to see what needs to be done.
3. Use your planning form to mark down the sequence of tomorrow's calls and any other work that must be done—such as phone calls.
4. Check your memo file for additional information you may need.
5. Put everything you will need in your briefcase or car.
6. Check your trunk file to make sure you have the necessary samples and brochures.

Preparation and paperwork are never as much fun as *selling*—but they are vital to your success. With the right amount of preparation, your sales day will be even more exciting.

ACCEPT THE HANDLING OF COMPLAINTS AS AN IMPORTANT PART OF YOUR JOB

Customer complaints are inevitable. No matter how you try, certain "gripes" will arise about you, your company, your product, and your service. These gripes can be controlled and handled swiftly with discretion and tact, or they can explode into a major crisis if allowed to get out of hand.

Nine out of ten grievances are little more than emotional outbursts. They stem from irritation or frustration, or from unfair or indifferent treatment—real or imagined.

The professional salesperson pinpoints the problem and brings it out in the open as fast as possible. The longer he or she lets it simmer, the higher the emotional flames are apt to rise.

One of the best ways to handle a grievance, of course, is to prevent it from happening in the first place. When you effectively service the account before *and after* the sale, you can avoid complaints. For example, you might even be able to spot—and do something about—possible quality or delivery problems before the customer does. That is smart insight, and it's good salesmanship. Also, knowing the other person's viewpoint and adjusting your tactics to it will solve a lot of problems.

Salesmanship is largely comprised of social interaction, the fine interplay between two or more human beings. It entails the understanding of each participant's viewpoint.

One of the best ways to zero in on the complainer's viewpoint is to empathize with him. Picture that person at his desk; imagine the pressures and frustrations he is enduring—then, picture yourself in his position. That "creative imagery" has a softening effect. It is like a handshake with a bitter opponent. (It is difficult to be antagonistic to a person whose hand you hold.)

Therefore, two important keys to handling complaints are to service the account and *prevent* the complaint from arising; and to understand the customer's viewpoint.

But it isn't always that easy. Complaints *will* arise and they are sometimes difficult to handle, even when you understand the complainer's viewpoint. In such a case, be fast and forthright. You move swiftly to prevent the complaint from spreading to others; and you are forthright by admitting blame (if you are wrong). (Of course, you correct the fault and take steps to prevent it from happening again.)

Last but not least is your own attitude about complaints. Recognize complaint handling as a part of your job—and use your sales techniques in handling the complaint, the complainer, and members of your backup team if they are involved.

KNOW YOUR PROSPECT'S ROUTINE
FOR PROCESSING A PURCHASE ORDER
—AND COOPERATE

Your prospect says: "I'll buy it. I'll write a purchase order requisition."

This agreement starts a series of events. It is the routine required for the issuance of a formal purchase order. It is important for you to understand each step and its purpose in the process. In some cases, you can speed things up and get that purchase order very quickly. In other cases, it is wise to let things take their natural course. A lot depends on the people involved.

One way to expedite the purchase order is to make sure the prospect's *requisition* contains all the necessary information. This reduces the time required by the Purchasing Department personnel to process the order. Here are some of the details needed for the average requisition:

1. A description and specifications of the product to be bought
2. The name of the manufacturer
3. The name of the supplier (when sold through a distributor or dealer)
4. The price of the product
5. The quantity discount
6. The net price per unit
7. The shipping point
8. The F.O.B. terms
9. The state sales tax (when applicable)
10. The approximate shipping weight
11. The shipping date
12. The approximate arrival date
13. Payment terms (such as thirty days net or 2 percent discount for payment within thirty days)
14. The guarantee of the product

(Note: If your company is the only producer of the item being purchased, it is a good idea to include a statement to that effect; otherwise, the Purchasing Department might be required to request quotations from other suppliers.)

The purchase requisition sometimes requires two or three signatures before being relayed to the Purchasing Department. Some requisitions are first sent to the Comptroller's office to make sure budgeted funds are available.

Some purchasing departments have buyers who are assigned to the purchase of certain product lines. The requisition for your product, therefore, may be first processed by a buyer and then sent for countersignature to the purchasing director (sometimes called a purchasing agent).

Some companies have rules that require requests for quotation for purchases that exceed a certain dollar amount. This rule applies even when there is only one source of supply. The request for quotation is sent by mail to the proposed vendor(s). The response from the vendor must be in writing and is usually done by returning the completed Request for Quotation form to the purchasing department.

When the purchase order is finally released, it carries with it an Acknowledgment form. This form should be filled out, signed by the vendor, and promptly returned to the purchasing department. It is a formal acceptance of the terms and conditions of the order.

Some purchase orders will designate the exact receiving point for the delivery of the material. In large companies, even the dock or door number is specified. Compliance with these instructions is good business—and good salesmanship. It is important to the purchasing company for correct handling of receivng department reports. It is important to the seller because the smooth handling of the receiving information will expedite payment of the invoice.

One of the most important items on a purchase order is the purchase order *number*. This identification must appear on all shipping papers and labels. It ties the requisition and purchase order to the receiving documents. In some cases, a friendly purchasing director or buyer will telephone the purchase order number to the vendor and then follow it up with the mailed purchase order form.

The delay caused by this routine may be frustrating to the eager sales representative awaiting the confirmation of a handsome order. When you are aware of the numerous steps required, you can understand the delay. You may, however, be able to speed up the process by exercising a certain amount of salesmanship on the people involved. Here are some suggestions:

1. As previously mentioned, help the prospect complete the requisition so that all necessary information is presented in one package to the purchasing department.
2. Make a tactful follow-up on the requisitioner (and/or his secretary) to make sure the requisition is expedited to the purchasing department.

3. Promptly return the Request for Quotation form and send with it a courteous, friendly letter to the purchasing director.

4. Make all personnel in the prospect's purchasing department feel important.

5. Don't be "pushy" or demanding. Resentment can create resistance—and resistance can cause delay.

6. If the climate is right, you can ask the buyer to telephone the purchase order number to you. Your reason for this request is to expedite the shipment for the advantage of the buyer—not the seller.

7. When you return the purchase order acknowledgment, write the buyer a "thank you" letter or note. You will be rewarded by his personal attention to subsequent purchase orders.

In summary, when you have a better understanding of the routine involved in processing a purchase order, you can follow good salesmanship principles all along the way. You can expedite those important purchase orders—and make friends as you do it. Also remember that your transaction with your buyer is not complete until the goods are delivered, the customer is satisfied, and the invoice is paid.

One final suggestion on this subject: Make sure you have done a complete job on your order and followed the suggestions for expediting it. Then *relax*. Don't sweat it. Let the paperwork process take its course. Go out and get more orders started. Don't waste time watching for the mail or listening for the telephone to ring.

Tips on Selling Through Dealers

Your company may assign you to supervise dealers in your geographic territory. The term "dealers" in this context includes any type of sales operation: dealer, distributor, or manufacturer's agent.

Many companies choose the direct sales type of distribution for the areas with the greatest potential, and then dealer coverage for the less profitable territories. And some companies select the nearest company sales representative to supervise the dealers. If such is the case with you, the tips in this chapter will help you on your supervisory assignment.

WHEN YOU SELL THROUGH DEALERS, TRAIN THE DEALER SALESPEOPLE

Many sales representatives sell through dealers as well as selling direct. When you *do* have dealers in your territory, you are, in effect, a sales manager—so *think* like a sales manager.

Even though those dealer salespeople are not on *your* payroll, they *are* representing you and your products. Make sure they do it right. This takes tact and diplomacy, but it will pay enormous dividends.

The average dealer is "multi-line," which means that he represents other companies as well as yours. You are therefore competing with the other manufacturers for a fair share of the dealer's selling time. You can get even more than your share when you offer sales training to the dealer's sales force. There are reasons for this.

1. A complete sales training program consists of six major segments:

- Product knowledge
- Markets and applications
- Territory management
- Time management
- Sales techniques
- Attitude

2. The average manufacturer trains its dealers only in products, and markets and applications. It also tries to develop attitude through incentives and sales meetings that are designed to motivate.

3. The average manufacturer does not offer to train its dealer salespeople in territory management, time management, and sales techniques because it assumes the established dealer knows these subjects and would resent outside training.

4. The dealer, on the other hand, presents his organization to the manufacturer as one that is trained, and professional. (It is on that basis that he got his contract with the manufacturer.) The dealer either doesn't know he needs help in territory management, time management, and sales techniques—or he is afraid to ask the manufacturer for it.

169

5. A training "vacuum" occurs when the dealer doesn't know that he needs help or is afraid to ask the manufacturer for it. The dealer volume suffers, the dealer salespeople sell "by guess and by God"—and you, as the sales manager in your territory, don't get full production from your dealer.

When you provide training in territory management, time management and sales techniques, the following occurs:

1. You develop a rapport with your dealer and his salespeople.
2. The dealer people, because of your help, give more attention and selling time to your product line.
3. You profit by increased sales and commissions.

Try this plan. It works. The next time you discuss with the dealer the features of an item in your line, say: "By the way, I've discovered some techniques that will sell this product real fast. Would you like to know about them?" That offer will be like a "breath of fresh air" to the dealer people. And it will launch a series of mini-discussions of a similar nature. You will be a hero to the dealer personnel—and you will profit from that extra effort.

KEEP THE LINES OF COMMUNICATION OPEN WITH YOUR DEALERS

Many of the tips offered so far apply to the handling of your dealers as well as your customers. The dealers are buyers as well as sellers of your products. They respond positively or negatively, exactly the way customers do.

Dealers like to be considered "part of the family." Keep them informed of your company's activities. Relay to them copies of company bulletins on products, testimonials, and success stories. In addition, send personal notes to dealer management and salespeople (refer to the tips in Chapter 9).

Conversely, see that communications *from* the dealers are relayed to the executives in your company who are most concerned about dealer operations. Be sure to follow up for replies. This is especially important if the feedback is a dealer complaint.

Communicate with your dealers as you do with customers. It's good salesmanship—and good sales management.

COACH THE DEALER SALESPEOPLE

Some dealer sales representatives may suggest that you make calls with them and watch them work. This is a compliment to you. Seize the opportunity. (Be sure, however, that the dealer management is agreeable to this field work.)

There are usually two reasons for making a call with another sales representative: One is for *you* to sell and the other person to observe, and the second is for the dealer salesperson to sell and for *you* to observe. This is called "coaching."

Before making the call, agree on who is to take the lead in the upcoming call. Lack of discussion and agreement beforehand can lead to confusion and embarrassment.

A particular situation may require you, the more experienced salesperson, to take the lead and make the sale. This is good for the sales volume—and for the dealer sales representative to see "how it is done." But it doesn't have the same long-lasting effects as the "coach and pupil" method.

The coach and pupil method is one of the best ways to train salespeople. Even blasé, experienced sales representatives can profit from the help of a good coach.

It isn't easy to be a good coach. It requires tact and a genuine desire to help. The first thing you need is a "track to run on"—a training program that works. It can be your company training program. Also, the tips in this book will augment any established course of instruction in salesmanship. It is helpful to use a prescribed vocabulary of terms when you coach. It saves a lot of time when both the coach and "pupil" understand the meaning of words such as the preapproach, the approach, the survey, probing questions, the close—and the hundreds of other words in "selling language."

During the joint sales call, you should try to remain the observer rather than an active participant. This requires a certain amount of self-discipline. Remember, the purpose of the coaching call is to strengthen the selling skills of your pupil—not to afford you the opportunity to demonstrate *your* selling skills. This takes much common sense because there may be times when you *must* take over during the sales interview to answer certain questions or even to rescue your pupil. Use your own judgment on when to do this, but try to let the inexperienced salesperson carry the ball as much as possible.

The critique or "curbstone conference" is usually held immediately after each joint sales call and always at the end of the coaching day. The development of a dialogue with the salesperson is a diplomatic way to open the discussion on his performance. A question from you such as "Jim, what are your impressions of that call we have just made?" will probably start him in a review of the *prospect's* reactions. Continue to ask questions directed to the *salesperson's* performance (in addition to the prospect's reactions). You can get him on that track by asking "How could you have answered his objection on price?" or other questions that will force him to review the call and *his own* actions in terms of good and poor tactics. You can help him along by being complimentary—when compliments are in order—and by being tactfully critical when discussing the negative parts of the presentation.

Obviously, you cannot use a checklist or make written notes during the joint sales call, but you *can* make *mental* notes of things to be discussed after the call. Keep it positive. Emphasize the good things. Get the new salesperson to realize the bad things and talk about them. Remember, the things that are not said can be dangerous.

CONDUCT DEALER SALES MEETINGS

Sales meetings can be training meetings. When they are properly conducted, they improve the sales performance of the participants. Develop a rapport with the dealer management and salespeople. Soon you will be invited to conduct some of the dealer's meetings. This affords you an excellent opportunity to increase your sales through that dealer by subtly training his salespeople.

Conduct a discussion-type meeting. This give everyone a chance to participate. It also permits you to be "low key"— acting as a participant rather than an instructor.

Choose and announce a subject well in advance of the meeting. Let's say you choose "Effective Closing Techniques" as the main theme. Announce the subject and state that you expect all attendees to share their expertise on "how to get the order." That invites anticipation and preparation.

Play on the strengths of the group. Develop a cross-table discussion on tested closing techniques. You, as the meeting leader, can be the quietest person in the room. You can exercise control by asking for opinions, redirecting questions, and tactfully interrupting the talkative members of the group. Try to get agreement on certain proven closing techniques and summarize them for all to use.

Before closing the meeting *on schedule*, get a meeting evaluation from each participant (see Figure 13–1). It will serve as an excellent "feedback," give each person an opportunity to suggest improvements, and guide your thinking as you plan the next meeting.

GENERAL TIPS
ON WORKING WITH DEALERS

Set Sales Objectives

Give the dealer management a quota (sales objective). Follow the traditional format for setting objectives. The quota should be made according to the following:

- Measurable (in terms everyone can agree on).
- Achievable (set at a reasonable, realistic level)
- Relevant (to the type of territory and its markets)
- Controllable (the dealer must have control over his performance)

Discuss the objectives frequently to emphasize the importance you place on them.

FIGURE 13-1 Meeting evaluation

```
                        MEETING EVALUATION


Please give us your opinion of this meeting.

How do you rate it?

   Excellent [  ]    Very good [  ]    Good [  ]    Fair [  ]    Poor [  ]

Did the meeting provide:

     (a) Considerable material and ideas you can use?          [  ]

     (b) Some material and ideas you can use?                  [  ]

     (c) No material and ideas you can use?                    [  ]

What did you like best about this meeting?
_____
_____
_____
_____
_____
_____
_____


What did you like least about this meeting?
_____
_____
_____
_____
_____
_____
_____
```

Use a "Bottom-Line" Approach

Many dealers think of the bottom line more frequently than company salespeople. This is because their profit from each transaction is more easily measured. Talk to the dealer in bottom-line language. He will quickly respond to it because the bottom line is his chief concern.

Work Closely
with Dealer Management

The owner of the dealership can learn a lot from you—and you from him. Keep him informed on your company's strategies and tactics that will concern him a his business.

Handle Commitments to Dealers
Promptly and Accurately

Remember that your dealer is your customer. Carry out all promises as quickly as possible. Tell the dealer if there are any changes in plans. You will build a climate of mutual respect and trust that will pay dividends to both parties.

Keep Your Management Informed
of Dealer Problems—and Progress

Make sure your corporate backup teams know about any pricing, quality, delivery, and service problems. Use the expertise at your home office to help you work with the dealer on those difficulties.

Likewise, keep your company management informed of sales and service accomplishments. For example, see that the dealer gets recognition for "big ticket" sales. Remember, the dealer wants to be part of the family. Award plaques, company newspaper articles, and letters from your company executives will make him feel that he is on your team.

Tips on
Working Trade Shows

For many companies in certain industries, trade shows are a very important vehicle for their sales promotion strategies. On a national basis, millions of dollars are spent every year for trade shows. One of the objectives, of course, is to develop leads which, in turn, create sales.

Unfortunately, many companies do not earn a good return on their investment. There are several reasons for this:

1. Poor preparation prior to the show
2. Untrained personnel in the booth
3. Poor follow-up of leads derived from the show

The tips in this chapter are offered to assist the salespeople who serve in the booth and follow up leads after the show.

PREPARE YOURSELF
BEFORE WORKING A TRADE SHOW

Your company may be one of the thousands of companies who exhibit their products at trade shows. If, you may be expected to help staff the booth for some of them.

Usually, the principal objective of a trade show is to generate sales through qualified leads. The second important objective is to exemplify the organization's "corporate image" by the quality of the booth and its personnel.

To obtain qualified leads, to properly represent your company, and to effectively follow up the leads takes planning, preparation, execution, and practice.

This tip or suggestion offers some help in preparing yourself for the booth assignment. Two subsequent tips cover booth behavior and following up the leads.

There are a variety of techniques for pre-show training. Some are provided, or should be provided, by your company. The balance are those techniques that a true professional will employ on his or her own initiative.

Pre-show training makes sense. If you have to take time from your territory to "work" on a trade show, you might as well do it right. It's more fun that way, and it can be a profitable experience.

Before practicing the techniques you plan to use at the show, it will be smart to discuss tactics and strategies with your manager and your peers. Here are some facts about most trade shows that should be considered when you plan yours:

1. The average time a prospect spends in a booth is only about five minutes.
2. You don't have time for a long-winded presentation.
3. A large percentage of the booth visitors will have no authority to buy.

These facts may not apply to trade shows in your industry. At any rate, it will be a good idea to discuss with your colleagues pertinent facts about visitors to your trade shows—and then plan your activities accordingly.

Some experienced trade show people spend the time available to the to qualify prospects. By tactful, preplanned questions, they find out first if the visitors have the authority to buy and, if so, exactly what they are interested in. Once these facts have been determined, they direct their efforts toward the subjects most interesting to the propsect. Many companies make their product presentations to qualified prospects in hospitality suites—away from the noise and confusion of the booth. The booth encounters, then, are simply designed to identify qualified prospects quickly; determine their needs; and extend invitations to presentations and further discussions.

One of the first things to do in your pre-show training is to examine the proposed layout of the booth. This will give you an idea of your working space. Then, imagine yourself performing that space.

It is also a good idea to review product literature. Practice handling it and retaining control of it as you point to one section and then another. (Remember: Many times a piece of literature stuffed in the visitor's hand becomes an immediate distraction and a possible hindrance to further dialogue.)

Practice demonstrating the products on display. Synchronize your physical movements with your verbal presentation. It's a good idea to practice before a mirror and with a tape recorder. You will be surprised how much this practice strengthens your demonstration.

Prepare a hand-held pad to use in getting complete information from prospects. That information should include the following:

1. Name of the visitor's company
2. Address and telephone number
3. Name and title of the visitor
4. Direct line, if applicable
5. Nature of the business
6. Equipment and supplies the visitor is currently using
7. Immediate interests and needs of the visitor
8. Name and location of the decision maker(s)

The act of writing creates an air of professionalism—and it pleases the visitor by indicating the importance of the information being given.

The use of the hand-held pad also serves three additional purposes:

1. It keeps you on track and saves your time.
2. It helps you "weed out" the idle curiosity seeker from the worthwhile prospects.
3. It makes every qualified lead more complete and intelligible—and increases the chances of effective follow-up.

Advice from corporate head quarters concerning the upcoming trade show should include the following

- Type and estimated size of the audience
- Corporate objectives for the show
- Products to be exhibited
- Size and shape of the booth
- Hotel and meal accomodation
- Your specific assignment of booth duty in terms days and hours

Also important in pre-show preparation are role plays with your peers. These can include the following:

- Using a sales brochure as a visual aid
- Getting information from the visitor and using the hand-held pad
- Devising preplanning questions
- Demonstrating the product

When you "act out" with a fellow salesperson the various situations that you anticipate will happen both the "salesperson" and the "prospect" benefit from the training.

Pre-show planning and training will make your booth assignment exciting and rewarding—and will make you look good in the eyes of your executives, peers, and visitors.

RULES FOR EFFECTIVE "BOOTH BEHAVIOR" WHEN WORKING A TRADE SHOW

This tip on booth behavior should be read in conjunction with the preceding tip, "Prepare Yourself Before Working at a Trade Show."

Your professional behavior at the trade show will exemplify your organization's corporate image. Conversely, poor behavior can have a strong, adverse effect on your investment of time and your company's heavy investment of dollars.

Professional booth behavior includes many things such as appearance, attitude, approach to visitors, conduct, tactful questioning, communicating, effective demonstrating, and gaining agreement to the desired action. This behavior applies to both work in the booth and in the hospitality suite (and in restaurants, when applicable). They can be summed up under the heading of "The Ensemble of Professionalism." That "ensemble" is what attracts people to your booth, holds them there, makes them want to give you information about themselves, their companies, and their needs, and makes them anxious to pursue your suggestions in greater detail. That "ensemble of professionalism" is made up of little things. Each "thing" seems insignificant when studied separately, but when combined, they make an effective presentation that will cause you to stand out and demand favorable attention.

To really appreciate the importance of that "ensemble," review some of your own experiences when visiting automobile dealerships, stores, or trade shows. Trade shows, in particular, offer excellent opportunities to view good and bad "ensembles" because of the number of booths and the great variances in the quality of salesmanship in evidence. You will profit from viewing those examples of good and bad performances. See yourself through the eyes of the visitor.

Your appearance is of great importance and is something that is seldom mentioned by your superiors and peers. It includes grooming as well as clothing. Study a salesperson who looks "well put together." Once again, you see a lot of little things: the right suit, carefully selected accessories, the coat buttoned (if coats are appropriate for the occasion), hair groomed, and everything freshly pressed and clean looking. That takes thought and good planning.

Your attitude is also of vital importance. It shows through in much that you say and do. Planning and preparing yourself for the booth assignment will help you create a good attitude for what you do there. Pride in yourself, your company, and your products are essential to good attitude—and pre-show training will help you acquire (or revive) that pride.

The style you use in the booth can differ from the style you use in the field. An aggressive, assertive approach to visitors in the booth is not as offensive as it might be in other situations. Once again, pre-show practice will help you develop the various approaches to prospects, governed by your own "gut" feeling for each case. Your conduct when "on display" must be exemplary. Refrain from snacking and smoking when on duty. Many people don't like smoking and smoker's breath. Don't sit or lean. Maintain an alert, erect posture—and don't congregate with colleagues in the booth. If this intensity of conduct is too difficult for you to maintain, arrange for more frequent "breaks." Your conduct in the booth is important, because someone is always watching.

Remember that one of your objectives is to obtain *qualified* leads. You do that by asking questions. The right questions develop a dialogue, and that dialogue, when carefully steered by you, can reveal vital information about the person, his company, and the company's needs. Ask open-ended questions that force complete replies. Closed questions can shut you off. For example, don't ask, "May I help you?" That's a closed question that is sometimes answered by "No, I'm just looking."

Questions that start with What, When, Where, How, Why, and Who are open-ended questions that cannot be answered by a simple "yes" or "no."

Program your brain with specific open-ended questions that are "tailored" to your booth assignment and objectives. The hand-held note pad previously mentioned could also contain a "prompter" list of preplanned questions designed to qualify the visitor.

Your skill as a communicator will also pay dividends in the booth. This includes nonverbal as well as verbal communication. Body language can play an important part in the dialogue. Good eye contact, for example, can express sincere interest and pleasure in the conversation. An erect posture and note-taking can also express that professional interest that will encourage more information from the visitor.

There is always a great deal of noise at trade shows, so in your verbal communication remember to speak up, speak clearly, and speak forcefully.

The use of the paraphrase is an effective technique for continuing the dialogue—for example, a statement such as "Mr. _____, a moment ago you said _____ _____ _____ _____. Will you give me more details on that?" The fact that you remembered the visitor's comment and referred back to it will encourage that person to divulge even more information.

Saying a person's name frequently is also a well-known conversation technique. First, be sure you have the visitor's name properly spelled and that you are pronouncing it correctly. Then, use it frequently. The use of the visitor's name can also be employed to signify the beginning of the next step in the dialogue. For example: "*Mr. Brown*, from what you have told me so far, I think we can help you with your problem. I suggest that we meet at your office, (etc., etc.)."

The *rewarding remark*, used frequently, will keep the dialogue going. Use remarks such as: "That's interesting," "That's good thinking," "Nice going," "I'll bet that paid off," and so on.

Effective demonstrating requires planning, preparation, and practice. Once again, role plays in the demonstration techniques during the pre-show training will help you perfect your demonstration technique.

Gaining agreement to the desired action can usually be accomplished by using a "closing question." Here is an example: "When may we demonstrate our _____ to your group?" (This is an open-ended question that requires a complete answer.) Preplanned questions of this type should be "programmed" into your brain so they can be used smoothly—and at the opportune time.

To the jaded trade show visitor, the booth behavior suggested in this tip will be like "a breath of fresh air." And, incidentally, many of the techniques described here need not be limited to trade shows. They are the techniques top performers use in *all* sales situations.

FOLLOW UP LEADS FROM TRADE SHOWS

In most cases, the payoff on trade show investment is the conversion of leads into sales.

This tip should be studied and practiced in conjunction with the tips entitled "Preparing Yourself before Working at a Trade Show" and Rules for Effective "Booth Behavior when Working a Trade Show."

This and the preceding tips on trade shows emphasize the need for pre-show training and professional action—the prime purpose being to get the most out of your investment of time and your company's heavy dollar investment. This is accomplished by carefully qualifying leads; and following up those leads.

Qualified is the key word here. When the contacts with booth visitors are properly handled, qualified leads are produced. The screening process at the booth makes the subsequent sales work easier. The "wheat" is separated from the "chaff" early in the booth encounter. It makes sense and it's good salesmanship.

If you are lucky, some of the leads you are assigned to follow might be those that you generated at the booth. That, of course, will make it much easier for you. Following up those leads will simply be a continuation of your earlier contacts.

In most cases, however, the leads you are given will have been started by another salesperson. Also, they may have been written in another part of the country. This, of course, makes the lead follow-up a little more difficult.

As suggested in the preceding tips on trade shows, the lead information should include the following:

1. Name of the visitor's company
2. Address and telephone number
3. Name and title of the visitor
4. Direct line, if applicable
5. Nature of the business
6. Equipment and supplies the visitor is currently using
7. Name and location of the decision maker(s)

(It is best, when possible, to have this information on a standardized lead form that is used company-wide for *all* trade shows. All salespeople, then, receive complete information regardless of the origin of the leads.)

The usual follow-up of a lead is accomplished in two steps: calling for an appointment and making the sales call.

When you arrange for an appointment, use the following example as a framework for your telephone call.

Greeting and identification. "Good morning, Mr. Barton. This is Bob Craig of _____ Corporation. Is it convenient for you to talk for just a moment?" *(Note: A seldom-used courtesy that helps the salesperson stand out.)*

(Pause and silence.)

Generating attention by telling something he did. "Mr. Barton, you attended the _____ trade show and indicated interest in our _____. That's what I'm calling about." *(Note the use of name.)*

Qualifying the prospect. Use probing questions as in the following two examples.

"Mr. Barton, what type of _____ are you using now?" (Ask this question only if this information is not on the lead form) "How often do you have jobs for that type of equipment?" (Ask this question if this information is not on the lead form.)

Qualifying the individual. Again, use probing questions. "Mr. Barton, are you the decision maker for this type of purchase, or will there be someone else involved?"

Selling the appointment. "Mr. Barton, the _____ is *compact, easy to handle,* and performs *all the functions.* It *costs only a fraction* of what you'd pay for a _____ type of unit. Herefore, you can get *more jobs done cheaper, faster,* and with *greater profit* to you." *(Note: After being satisfied of a good lead, the salesperson proceeds to sell the appointment. Be sure to point out the good features as well as the benefits of these features.)*

"Mr. Barton, your neighbor down the street, the _____ company, has three of our _____ in their service department. Mr. Miller, the service manager, will be glad to show us a unit in action." (A success story.)

Asking for the desired action. "When may I come in to see you and _____?" (This is the closing question.)

(Pause and silence.)

Closing the telephone call. "Thank you, Mr. Barton. I shall be at your office at 10 o'clock tomorrow morning. Good bye, sir." (The salesperson waits for Mr. Barton to hang up.)

After the appointment is made, the sales call follows the usual format for an effective, professional sales interview:

1. Gain favorable attention
2. Develop a dialogue
3. Make the proposal
4. Handle questions and objections
5. Ask for the order

The conversion of leads into sales is the main purpose of the trade show. The three tips on trade show coverage will help make it happen.

15

Put It All Together

This book has "dissected" for you the framework of a professional development program. Each major segment was examined: product knowledge, market and application knowledge, territory management, time management, sales techniques, and attitude.

It has further dissected the four methods of contacting customers and prospects:

- face-to-face
- by telephone
- by mail
- by formal written proposal

It has placed the greatest emphasis on sales techniques, the psychological concepts of persuasive selling, and attitude building.

186

The tips in this book are offered to give you a broad perspective on what a successful salesperson needs to know and do. Those tips will reinforce the training your company has already provided.

Now the "dissection" is over and your reassembling task begins.

PUT IT ALL TOGETHER

Put all of what you have learned into a "Ensemble of Professionalism." Be a professional salesperson "on stage" in contact with your prospect and customer. Be like a professional actor as you use your stage props (sale tools, body language, and selling sentences. Be an "ensemble of professionalism" in action—effective action.

Plan your presentation from your entrance to your exit. Gain immediate favorable attention by establishing a dialogue—not a monologue.

Be clean and neat—and choose the correct clothing and accessories. Be courteous but not timid, confident but not cocky.

Handle your sales tools and visuals with practiced smoothness. Time your verbal presentations with your visuals.

Handle objections and put-offs with thoughtful consideration. Reply to them with confidence, good eye contact, testimonials, and success stories.

Your ensemble of practiced, confident salesmanship (coupled with a good, worthwhile proposition) will influence the emotions as well as the practical sense of the buyer. It will make him *want* to buy from *you*.

Put all those little things together. You will be pleased with the profitable results, and you will find those results satisfying and rewarding.

Refer to this book again and again as you advance up the promotional ladder. It will be most helpful as you train, coach, and supervise others.

Index

190